APR 22 2003

D1399351

DISCARDED
From the Nashville Public
Library

Property of
Nashville Public Library
615 Church St., Nashville, TN 37219

Luscious Mousse Tartlets
recipe, page 8

HERSHEY'S

CHOCOLATE
for EVERY SEASON

Meredith® Books

Des Moines, Iowa

Chocolate Truffles
(recipe, page 78)

Credits

Produced by:
Meredith® Books and
Meredith Integrated Marketing,
1716 Locust Street,
Des Moines, IA 50309-3023.

Meredith Books
Editor: Chuck Smothermon
Design Production: Studio P2
Proofreaders: Marcy Hall,
    Beth Popplewell

Editor in Chief:
    James D. Blume
Design Director:
    Matt Strelecki
Managing Editor:
    Gregory H. Kayko
Executive Food Editor:
    Jennifer Dorland Darling

Director, Retail Sales and
    Marketing: Terry Unsworth
Director, Sales, Special
    Markets: Rita McMullen
Director, Sales, Premiums:
    Michael A. Peterson
Director, Production:
    Douglas M. Johnston

Vice President, General Manager:
    Jamie L. Martin

greetings from HERSHEY'S

Each season offers its own charm and rhythm. The cold, pristine days of winter are followed by gentle spring rains. We slow our pace under the hot summer sun, then pick it up again as autumn promises a return to school and routine. In addition, throughout the year we gather with family and friends to rejoice and celebrate birthdays, anniversaries and special holidays.

As the days of the year unfold, turn to *HERSHEY'S Chocolate for Every Season* for a luscious dessert or treat befitting the occasion. In February, delight the special person in your life with Dark-Chocolate Truffle Cake. Before the fireworks on the Fourth of July, scoop up bowls of Chocolate-Cherry Ice Cream. And for the holidays, share a batch of Peanut Butter-Marshmallow Fudge with loved ones.

With this collection of kitchen-tested recipes and the quality products from HERSHEY'S and BLUE DIAMOND, success and good times are guaranteed year-round.

For more recipes, visit us at **www.hersheykitchens.com** *and* **www.bluediamondgrowers.com**

HERSHEY'S

CHOCOLATE for EVERY SEASON

This seal assures you that every recipe in *HERSHEY'S Chocolate for Every Season* has been tested in the *Better Homes and Gardens®* Test Kitchen. This means that each recipe is practical and reliable and meets high standards of taste appeal.

Originally published as *Hershey's® Celebrates Each Season.*

Copyright © 2001, 2000 Hershey Foods Corporation and Meredith Corporation.
All rights reserved. Printed in China.
First Edition.
Library of Congress Catalog Control Number: 2001130201
ISBN: 0-696-21338-9

BLUE DIAMOND® and the BLUE DIAMOND® design are registered trademarks
owned by the California Almond Growers Exchange.

If you would like to purchase any Meredith books, check wherever quality books
are sold. Visit our website at meredithbooks.com.

Pictured on front cover: Easy Chocolate-Orange Cake (recipe, page 24)

Add glamour and style

to winter holidays and feasts

with your best china, candles and

these ultra-rich tortes, tarts and

other sweet creations.

winter elegance with chocolate

Mint-Brownie Dessert (recipe, page 6)

mint-brownie dessert

Tint the creamy mint topping to suit the occasion—green for St. Patrick's Day or pink for Valentine's Day (photo, pages 4–5).

prep time: 30 minutes • baking time: 20 minutes • chilling time: 2 hours

Nonstick cooking spray
5 bars (1 ounce each) HERSHEY'S Semi-Sweet Baking Chocolate, divided
¼ cup (½ stick) butter
½ cup sugar
1 egg
½ teaspoon vanilla extract
⅔ cup all-purpose flour
2 tablespoons HERSHEY'S Cocoa
½ teaspoon baking powder
¼ teaspoon baking soda

⅓ cup milk
1 package (8 ounces) cream cheese, softened
¾ cup sugar
½ teaspoon peppermint extract
3 cups (8 ounces) frozen non-dairy whipped topping, thawed
Few drops food coloring (optional)
1 teaspoon shortening
Crushed starlight mints (optional)

1. Heat oven to 350°F. Lightly coat the bottom and sides of 9-inch springform pan with nonstick cooking spray. Set aside.

2. Combine 3 bars of the baking chocolate and the butter in medium saucepan; stir over low heat just until melted. Remove from heat. Stir in the ½ cup sugar. Add egg and vanilla, beating lightly with wooden spoon just until combined. Stir together flour, cocoa, baking powder and baking soda. Add flour mixture and milk alternately to chocolate mixture, stirring just until combined after each addition. Pour into prepared springform pan. Place pan on shallow baking pan. Bake about 20 minutes or until wooden pick inserted near center comes out clean. Cool in pan on wire rack.

3. Beat cream cheese and the ¾ cup sugar in medium bowl on medium speed of mixer until smooth. Stir in peppermint extract. Fold in whipped topping; tint with food coloring, if desired. Spread evenly over cooled brownie in pan.

4. Cover; refrigerate at least 2 hours or up to 24 hours. To serve, use narrow metal spatula to loosen edge; remove sides of pan. Cut into wedges.

5. Place remaining 2 bars (2 ounces) baking chocolate and the shortening in small microwave-safe bowl. Microwave at HIGH (100%) for 1 minute; stir. Microwave an additional 15 seconds at a time, stirring after each heating, until melted and smooth. Drizzle melted chocolate over wedges. Sprinkle with crushed candy, if desired.

Makes 12 to 16 servings.

dark-chocolate truffle cake

prep time: 45 minutes • baking time: 40 minutes
cooling time: 2 hours 20 minutes • chilling time: 4 hours
standing time: 30 minutes

2 cups sliced BLUE DIAMOND
   Almonds, toasted
   and finely chopped
¼ cup (½ stick) butter, melted
1 cup sifted HERSHEY'S
   Cocoa
⅔ cup sugar
2 cups (12-ounce package)
   HERSHEY'S Semi-Sweet
   Chocolate Chips

1 cup whipping cream
½ cup (1 stick) butter, cut up
6 eggs
1 teaspoon vanilla extract
⅓ cup all-purpose flour
¼ cup sugar
½ cup whipping cream
   Whole BLUE DIAMOND
   Almonds

1. Heat oven to 325°F. Stir together the 2 cups almonds and the ¼ cup melted butter. Let stand for 10 minutes. Press onto bottom and 1½ inches up the sides of 9-inch springform pan. Set aside.

2. Stir together cocoa and the ⅔ cup sugar in a heavy, medium saucepan; stir in chocolate chips, the 1 cup whipping cream and the ½ cup butter. Heat over low heat just until chocolate and butter are melted, stirring constantly. Cover surface; cool to room temperature.

3. Beat eggs and vanilla in large bowl on low speed of mixer until combined. Add flour and the ¼ cup sugar. Beat on high speed about 10 minutes or until slightly thick. Fold about one-fourth of the egg mixture into chocolate mixture. Fold chocolate mixture into remaining egg mixture.

4. Spread batter into the prepared pan. Place pan on shallow baking pan. Bake 40 to 45 minutes or until slightly puffed about 1½ inches in from outer edge (center will be slightly soft). Cool in pan on a wire rack for 20 minutes. Loosen cake from sides of pan; remove sides of the pan. Cool 2 to 3 hours more. (Cake may dip slightly in center after cooling.) Refrigerate for at least 4 hours or up to 24 hours.

5. To serve, let stand at room temperature 30 minutes. Meanwhile, pour the ½ cup whipping cream into chilled medium bowl; beat with chilled beaters on medium speed of mixer just until stiff peaks form. Spoon whipped cream into a decorating bag fitted with a medium star tip (about ¼-inch opening). Pipe whipped cream on top of cake. Garnish with whole almonds. Cover and refrigerate leftover cake.

Makes 16 to 20 servings.

luscious mousse tart

You can also garnish this rich tart with whipped cream and almonds.

prep time: 1¼ hours • chilling time: 3 hours

¾ cup all-purpose flour
½ cup sifted powdered sugar
⅓ cup HERSHEY'S Cocoa
¼ teaspoon salt
⅛ teaspoon baking soda
⅓ cup cold butter
3 to 4 tablespoons ice water

2 cups (12-ounce package) HERSHEY'S Semi-Sweet Chocolate Chips
1 teaspoon vanilla extract
2 cups whipping cream
2 tablespoons granulated sugar

1. For crust, stir together flour, powdered sugar, cocoa, salt and baking soda. Using a pastry blender, cut in butter until pieces are pea-size. Sprinkle 1 tablespoon of the water over part of the mixture; gently toss with a fork. Repeat moistening dough, using 1 tablespoon of the water at a time, until all dough is moistened. Form dough into a ball. Cover; refrigerate for 30 to 60 minutes or until dough is easy to handle.

2. Heat oven to 450°F. On a lightly floured surface, slightly flatten dough ball. Roll dough from center to edges into a circle 12 inches in diameter. Place pastry in a 9- or 10-inch fluted tart pan with a removable bottom. Press pastry into fluted side of tart pan; trim edge and prick bottom and side. Line with double thickness of foil. Bake 8 minutes; remove foil. Bake 4 to 5 minutes more or until dry and set. Cool on wire rack.

3. Meanwhile, for mousse, combine chocolate chips and vanilla in a food processor bowl. Bring 1 cup of the whipping cream just to boiling in a heavy small saucepan. With processor running, gradually add hot cream; process until chocolate is melted and smooth. Transfer to a large bowl. Cool to room temperature, stirring occasionally.

4. Combine remaining 1 cup whipping cream and the granulated sugar in medium bowl; beat until soft peaks form (tips curl). Fold whipped cream into chocolate mixture. Refrigerate until mixture mounds (about 20 minutes), stirring occasionally. Spoon mousse into tart shell, mounding mixture high in shell. Cover; refrigerate 3 to 6 hours or until set.

Makes 8 servings.

Luscious Mousse Tartlets: Prepare crust as above, except divide dough ball into 8 portions. On a lightly floured surface, roll each portion into a circle 4½ to 5 inches in diameter. Place pastry circles in eight 3½- to 4-inch fluted tart pans with removable bottoms. Continue as above. Makes 8.

Luscious Mousse Tartlets
(To make the garnish, see tip on page 16)

tiramisu torte

prep time: 45 minutes • baking time: per angel cake package directions

1 package (15 to 16 ounces) angel cake mix
⅓ cup HERSHEY'S Cocoa
1 package (8 ounces) cream cheese, softened
2 cups whipping cream, divided
⅔ cup sifted powdered sugar
3 tablespoons HERSHEY'S Cocoa

1 tablespoon instant espresso powder or instant coffee crystals
1 bar (1 ounce) HERSHEY'S Semi-Sweet Baking Chocolate, coarsely grated
½ cup sliced BLUE DIAMOND Almonds, toasted

1. Prepare cake mix according to package directions, except sift the ⅓ cup cocoa and stir into dry ingredients. After spooning cake batter into pan, gently cut through the batter with a narrow metal spatula to eliminate any air bubbles. Bake cake as directed. Invert cake in pan on heat-proof funnel or bottle. Cool completely. Carefully run knife along sides of pan to loosen cake; remove from pan.

2. For filling, beat cream cheese in large bowl on medium speed of mixer until smooth. Add 1 cup of the whipping cream, the powdered sugar, the 3 tablespoons cocoa and the espresso powder or coffee crystals. Beat until fluffy and smooth. Using same beaters, beat remaining 1 cup whipping cream until stiff peaks form. Fold whipped cream into cream cheese mixture. Fold grated chocolate into cream cheese mixture.

3. To assemble, cut cake horizontally into 3 layers. Place bottom layer on a serving platter. Spread with 1 cup of the filling. Repeat layering with second cake layer and another 1 cup of the filling. Top with third cake layer. Spread remaining filling over cake. Sprinkle almonds over top of cake. Refrigerate until serving time.

Makes 10 servings.

toasting almonds
Enhance the texture and nutty flavor of BLUE DIAMOND almonds by toasting them. Heat oven to 350°F. Spread the almonds in a thin layer in a shallow baking pan. Bake for 5 to 10 minutes or until almonds are light golden brown, stirring occasionally; cool before using.

chocolate-banana celebration cake

From December 26 to January 1, African-Americans honor their heritage in a celebration called Kwanzaa. This luscious banana-chocolate-coconut cake makes a satisfying dessert to serve at family and community gatherings throughout the seven-day festival—or at any other celebration.

prep time: 25 minutes • baking time: 50 minutes

⅔ cup butter, softened
1½ cups sugar
1 teaspoon vanilla extract
2 eggs
2 cups all-purpose flour
¾ cup HERSHEY'S Cocoa
1½ teaspoons baking soda
1 teaspoon salt
1 container (16 ounces) dairy sour cream

¾ cup mashed banana
1 cup MOUNDS Sweetened Coconut Flakes
½ to 1 teaspoon freshly grated orange peel (optional)
Creamy Vanilla Frosting (recipe follows)
Additional coconut, orange peel and banana slices* for garnish (optional)

1. Heat oven to 350°F. Grease and flour 12-cup fluted tube pan. Set aside.

2. Beat butter, sugar and vanilla in large bowl on medium speed of mixer until creamy. Beat in eggs, one at a time, beating 1 minute after each addition. Stir together flour, cocoa, baking soda and salt; add alternately with sour cream to butter mixture, beating on low speed after each addition just until combined. Stir in mashed banana, coconut and the ½ to 1 teaspoon orange peel, if desired. Pour batter into prepared pan.

3. Bake 50 to 55 minutes or until wooden pick inserted in center comes out clean. Cool 10 minutes; remove from pan to wire rack. Cool completely.

4. To serve, prepare Creamy Vanilla Frosting; spoon over cake. Garnish with additional coconut, orange peel and banana slices, if desired.

Makes about 12 servings.

Creamy Vanilla Frosting: Beat 1 cup sifted powdered sugar, 2 tablespoons softened butter and ½ teaspoon vanilla extract in small bowl on medium speed of mixer until blended. Gradually add 1 tablespoon milk, beating well. Add additional milk, ¼ teaspoon at a time, until of desired consistency. Makes about ⅓ cup.

*Note: To keep the banana slices from browning, dip them in lemon juice.

black forest shortcakes

After battling the crowds at the Presidents' Day sales, whip up this mouthwatering dessert—chocolate biscuits smothered with sweet dark cherries and whipped topping.

prep time: 20 minutes   •   baking time: 8 minutes

1⅔ cups all-purpose flour	¾ cup milk
½ cup HERSHEY'S Cocoa	Sugar
⅓ cup sugar	Cherry Sauce
1 tablespoon baking powder	(recipe follows)
¼ teaspoon salt	Frozen non-dairy whipped
½ cup (1 stick) butter	topping, thawed
1 beaten egg	

1. Heat oven to 450°F. Lightly grease two baking sheets. Set aside.

2. For shortcakes, combine flour, cocoa, the ⅓ cup sugar, the baking powder and salt in large bowl. Using a pastry blender, cut in butter until mixture resembles coarse crumbs. Combine egg and milk; add all at once to flour mixture and stir just until moistened. Drop dough into 18 portions on prepared baking sheets. Sprinkle with additional sugar. Bake about 8 minutes or until wooden pick inserted in centers comes out clean. Cool slightly on a wire rack.

3. Meanwhile, prepare Cherry Sauce. To serve, spoon about half of the sauce into six dessert dishes. Place three shortcakes in each dish. Spoon remaining warm sauce over shortcakes. Spoon whipped topping onto each serving.

Makes 6 servings.

Cherry Sauce: Combine ¼ cup sugar and 1 tablespoon cornstarch in medium saucepan. Add 2 cups fresh or frozen (not thawed) pitted dark sweet cherries and ½ cup apple juice. Cook and stir over medium heat until bubbly. Cook and stir 2 minutes more. Remove from heat. Stir in ¼ teaspoon almond extract. Let stand for 15 minutes. Serve warm. Makes 1½ cups.

CHOCOLATE IN THE ARMY

During World War II, chocolate provided nourishment as well as morale for the Allied Armed Forces. Throughout the war, the U.S. government allocated valuable shipping space to ensure a steady supply of cocoa beans and chocolate for the troops. Many times pocket chocolate bars sustained soldiers until more food was available. And today, U.S. Army D-rations contain three 4-ounce chocolate bars.

Black Forest Shortcakes

midnight chocolate cake

prep time: 1 hour • baking time: 1 hour 20 minutes • chilling time: 4 hours

3	eggs	3	cups sifted cake flour
2¾	cups sugar		or 2¾ cups sifted
1	teaspoon vanilla extract		all-purpose flour
¾	cup cooking oil	¾	teaspoon baking powder
1¾	cups water	½	teaspoon salt
1½	cups HERSHEY'S Dutch	¼	teaspoon baking soda
	Processed Cocoa or		Chocolate Filling
	HERSHEY'S Cocoa		(recipe, page 15)
			Chocolate Buttercream
			(recipe, page 15)

1. Grease and flour 10-inch springform pan; set aside. Heat oven to 325°F. Beat eggs, sugar and vanilla in a large bowl on high speed of mixer for 5 minutes or until light and fluffy. With mixer running, slowly add oil, beating until combined.

2. Bring water to boiling; gradually add to cocoa in a small bowl, stirring until smooth. Beat cocoa mixture into egg mixture. Set aside.

3. Stir together flour, baking powder, salt and baking soda. Add flour mixture to egg mixture, beating on low speed of mixer just until smooth and scraping sides of bowl occasionally. Pour batter into prepared pan.

4. Bake 1 hour 20 minutes to 1 hour 40 minutes or until wooden pick inserted near center comes out clean. Cool in pan on wire rack 20 minutes. Loosen cake from sides of pan; remove sides of pan. Carefully remove cake from bottom of pan. Cool cake completely on wire rack. Clean and reassemble pan.

5. Prepare Chocolate Filling. To assemble cake, use a serrated knife to trim top of cake to make it even. Split cake horizontally into three layers. Place first layer in the bottom of the springform pan. Pour half of the filling on top. Place second cake layer over filling. Pour in remaining filling; top with third cake layer. Cover; refrigerate 3 hours or until firm.

6. Run a hot knife or narrow metal spatula around edge of pan. Invert cake onto a serving plate; remove pan. Prepare Chocolate Buttercream; frost cake top and sides. Refrigerate until serving time.

Makes 16 servings.

Chocolate Filling: Microwave ⅔ cup HERSHEY'S Semi-Sweet Chocolate Chips in small, microwave-safe bowl at HIGH (100%) 1 minute; stir. Microwave an additional 15 seconds at a time, stirring after each heating, until chips are melted and smooth; let cool. Combine ⅓ cup sugar and 1 envelope unflavored gelatin in medium saucepan. Stir in ½ cup cream sherry or milk, ½ cup water and 5 slightly beaten egg yolks. Cook and stir over medium heat until mixture thickens slightly and bubbles just around edge. Transfer to large bowl. Add melted chocolate to egg mixture; beat on low speed of mixer until combined. Cover; cool for 30 minutes. Wash and dry beaters. Beat 1⅓ cups whipping cream and 1 teaspoon vanilla extract in medium bowl on low speed of mixer until soft peaks form; fold into egg mixture. Cover; refrigerate about 1 hour or until mounds when spooned, gently stirring occasionally. Makes 3½ cups.

Chocolate Buttercream: Microwave ⅔ cup HERSHEY'S Semi-Sweet Chocolate Chips in small microwave-safe bowl at HIGH (100%) for 1 minute; stir. Microwave an additional 15 seconds at a time, stirring after each heating, until chips are melted and smooth; let cool. Beat 2½ cups sifted powdered sugar and 1¼ cups (2½ sticks) softened butter on low speed of mixer until creamy. Add ¾ cup shortening; beat until smooth. Stir in melted chocolate and 1 teaspoon vanilla extract. Makes 4 cups.

chocolate-cream cheese pie

prep time: 30 minutes • chilling time: 7 hours

1 cup graham cracker crumbs	½ cup whipping cream
⅓ cup granulated sugar	2 packages (8 ounces each) cream cheese, softened
⅓ cup HERSHEY'S Cocoa	
⅓ cup butter, melted	1¼ cups sifted powdered sugar
1 cup HERSHEY'S Semi-Sweet Chocolate Chips	1 tablespoon vanilla extract

1. For crust, combine cracker crumbs, granulated sugar and cocoa; stir in melted butter until evenly moistened. Press evenly into a 9-inch pie plate. Refrigerate about 1 hour or until firm.

2. For filling, combine chocolate chips and whipping cream in a heavy medium saucepan. Cook and stir over medium heat until melted and smooth. Cool just to lukewarm.

3. Meanwhile, beat cream cheese, powdered sugar and vanilla on medium speed of mixer until combined. Beat in chocolate mixture. Spoon into crust. Cover; refrigerate at least 6 hours or up to 2 days.

Makes 8 servings.

fudgy mocha-almond pie

prep time: 45 minutes • baking time: 40 minutes • cooling time: 1 hour

⅓ cup butter
⅔ cup sugar
½ cup HERSHEY'S Cocoa
2 teaspoons instant espresso powder or instant coffee crystals
3 eggs
1 cup light corn syrup
¼ teaspoon salt

1 cup slivered BLUE DIAMOND Almonds, toasted
1 unbaked purchased refrigerated 9-inch piecrust (½ of a 15-ounce package)
Coffee Whipped Cream (recipe below)

1. Heat oven to 350°F. Melt butter in a medium saucepan over low heat; add sugar, cocoa and espresso powder or coffee crystals, stirring until combined. Remove from heat; set aside.

2. Combine eggs, corn syrup and salt in medium bowl. Add cocoa mixture, stirring until combined. Stir in almonds. Pour into unbaked piecrust. Cover edge of pie with foil to prevent overbrowning. Bake for 25 minutes; remove foil. Bake 15 minutes more. Cool on a wire rack for 1 hour. Refrigerate until serving time. Prepare Coffee Whipped Cream; serve with pie.

Makes 10 servings.

Coffee Whipped Cream: Combine ½ cup whipping cream, 1 tablespoon coffee liqueur or strong coffee (if desired) and 1 tablespoon powdered sugar in small chilled bowl; beat on medium speed of mixer until soft peaks form. Makes 1 cup.

---

versatile marbleized chocolate cutouts

Dress up desserts of all types with easy-to-make cutouts (such as the star shape shown on page 9). Place 1 cup HERSHEY'S Premier White Chips and 1 cup HERSHEY'S Semi-Sweet or Milk Chocolate Chips in separate, small microwave-safe bowls. Microwave at HIGH (100%) 1 minute; stir. If necessary, microwave at HIGH an additional 15 seconds or until melted and smooth when stirred.

Alternately pour melted chips onto wax paper-lined cookie sheet to create marbled effect; spread with metal spatula into 9- to 10-inch square. Refrigerate 3 to 5 minutes or just until mixture begins to set. Press tiny cookie cutter into chip mixture, pressing cutter through to bottom. Do not try to separate at this time. Cover; refrigerate several hours or until very firm. Carefully peel wax paper away; gently separate cutouts. Place cutouts on tray; refrigerate until ready to use as garnish.

Fudgy Mocha-Almond Pie

brownie trifle

Bring a touch of elegance to your next gathering with this make-ahead dessert—brownies soaked in coffee liqueur and layered with creamy chocolate pudding and almonds.

prep time: 35 minutes • baking time: 20 minutes • chilling time: 4 hours

⅔ cup sugar
⅓ cup butter
⅓ cup HERSHEY'S Cocoa
1 egg
½ teaspoon vanilla extract
⅔ cup all-purpose flour
½ teaspoon baking powder
⅛ teaspoon baking soda
½ cup milk
1 cup HERSHEY'S MINI CHIPS Semi-Sweet Chocolate, divided

¼ cup coffee liqueur or ¼ cup strong coffee plus 1 teaspoon sugar
1 package (4-serving size) instant chocolate pudding mix
3 cups (8 ounces) frozen non-dairy whipped topping, thawed
½ cup sliced BLUE DIAMOND Almonds

1. Heat oven to 350°F. Grease 9x9x2-inch baking pan. Set aside.

2. For brownies, combine sugar, butter and cocoa in large saucepan; heat, stirring constantly, over medium heat until butter melts. Remove from heat. Add egg and vanilla. Beat lightly on low speed of mixer just until combined. Combine flour, baking powder and baking soda. Add flour mixture and milk alternately to chocolate mixture, beating after each addition. Stir in ½ cup of the small chocolate chips. Pour batter into prepared pan.

3. Bake about 20 minutes or until wooden pick inserted near center comes out clean. Remove from oven. Using a fork, prick top of warm brownies at 1-inch intervals. Brush with coffee liqueur or mixture of coffee and sugar. Cool completely in pan on wire rack. Cut brownies into 1-inch pieces; set aside.

4. Prepare pudding mix according to package directions for making pie, except don't chill after beating. Stir in remaining ½ cup small chocolate chips.

5. Arrange half of the brownie pieces on bottom of 2-quart glass or clear plastic serving bowl. Layer with half of the pudding and half of the whipped topping. Sprinkle with half of the almonds. Repeat layers, ending with almonds. Cover; refrigerate at least 4 hours or up to 24 hours.

Makes 8 servings.

mocha-almond torte

Decked out in a glossy glaze and toasted almonds, this flourless cake steals the show at any holiday gala.

prep time: 25 minutes • baking time: 40 minutes • chilling time: 4 hours

2 cups sliced BLUE DIAMOND Almonds, toasted, divided

1⅓ cups HERSHEY'S Semi-Sweet Chocolate Chips

¾ cup sugar

½ cup HERSHEY'S Cocoa

1 tablespoon instant coffee crystals

1 teaspoon baking powder

¼ teaspoon baking soda

5 eggs

1 teaspoon vanilla extract

Mocha Glaze (recipe below)

1. Measure your food processor bowl to make sure it has a capacity of at least 3½ cups. Heat oven to 325°F. Grease and flour 9-inch springform pan. Set aside.

2. Combine 1½ cups of the almonds, the chocolate chips, sugar, cocoa, coffee crystals, baking powder and baking soda in food processor bowl. Cover and process about 1 minute or until nuts and chips are finely ground, stopping once and pushing mixture down. Add eggs and vanilla. Cover and process about 45 seconds or until nearly smooth.

3. Pour batter into prepared pan. Bake 40 to 45 minutes or until wooden pick inserted near center comes out nearly clean. Cool in pan on wire rack for 10 minutes. Loosen torte from sides of pan; remove sides of pan. Cool completely on wire rack.

4. Place torte on serving platter. Prepare Mocha Glaze; pour over cake, allowing it to drizzle down sides. Sprinkle remaining ½ cup almonds over top. Cover; refrigerate at least 4 hours. When serving, clean knife between cuts.

Makes 16 servings.

Mocha Glaze: Combine ⅔ cup HERSHEY'S Semi-Sweet Chocolate Chips and ¼ cup (½ stick) butter in heavy small saucepan. Over low heat, stir frequently until melted and smooth; remove from heat. Dissolve ¼ teaspoon instant coffee crystals in 1 tablespoon hot water. Stir coffee and 2 teaspoons light corn syrup into chocolate mixture, stirring until smooth. Let cool 10 to 15 minutes or until slightly thickened. Makes ⅔ cup.

springtime
cakes for
celebrations

Special get-togethers are as much a part

of spring as daffodils and gentle breezes.

Bake a festive cake for Mother's Day,

a graduation buffet or any other

notable occasion during this season.

Chocolate Pound Cake (recipe, page 22)

chocolate pound cake

For an extra-special touch, serve slices of this rich pound cake with fresh berries and a chocolate topper. Simply fold a tablespoon or two of sifted HERSHEY'S Cocoa into sweetened whipped cream (photo, pages 20–21).

prep time: 25 minutes • standing time: 30 minutes • baking time: 1 hour

½ cup (1 stick) butter	¼ teaspoon baking powder
3 eggs	¼ teaspoon baking soda
½ cup dairy sour cream	1¼ cups sugar
1¼ cups all-purpose flour	1 teaspoon vanilla extract
⅓ cup HERSHEY'S Cocoa	

1. Let butter, eggs and sour cream stand at room temperature 30 minutes. Heat oven to 325°F. Grease and lightly flour 9x5x3-inch loaf pan. Set aside.

2. Stir together flour, cocoa, baking powder and baking soda in medium bowl. Beat butter in large bowl on medium speed of mixer 30 seconds. Gradually add sugar, beating about 10 minutes or until very light and fluffy. Beat in vanilla. Add eggs, one at a time, beating 1 minute after each. Add flour mixture and sour cream alternately to beaten mixture, beating after each addition just until combined. Pour into prepared pan.

3. Bake 60 to 70 minutes or until wooden pick inserted in center comes out clean. Cool in pan on wire rack 10 minutes; remove from pan to wire rack. Cool completely.

Makes 10 to 12 servings.

fiesta fantasy cake

prep time: 40 minutes • baking time: 30 minutes • chilling time: 2½ hours

2 cups sifted cake flour or 1¾ cups sifted all-purpose flour	1 tablespoon coffee liqueur or strong coffee
½ cup HERSHEY'S Dutch Processed Cocoa	½ teaspoon vanilla extract
2 teaspoons baking soda	1 container (8 ounces) dairy sour cream
¼ teaspoon salt	¾ cup boiling water
2 cups packed brown sugar	Chocolate Mousse (recipe, page 23)
⅔ cup butter, softened	Chocolate Frosting (recipe, page 23)
3 eggs	

1. Heat oven to 350°F. Grease and flour two 9x1½-inch round cake pans. Combine flour, cocoa, baking soda and salt. Set aside.

2. Beat brown sugar and butter in large bowl on low to medium speed of mixer until combined. Add eggs, one at a time, beating well after each addition. Beat in coffee liqueur or coffee and vanilla. Add flour mixture and sour cream alternately to sugar mixture, beating after each addition just until combined. Stir in boiling water until blended. Pour into prepared pans.

3. Bake 30 to 35 minutes or until wooden pick inserted near centers comes out clean. Cool in pans on wire racks 10 minutes; remove from pans to wire racks. Cool completely.

4. Prepare Chocolate Mousse. Split each cake layer horizontally to make four layers total. Place one layer on serving plate; spread with one-third of the mousse (about 1 cup). Repeat layering with two of the remaining layers and remaining mousse. Place remaining cake layer on top. Prepare Chocolate Frosting; frost cake top and sides.

5. Cover; refrigerate at least 2 hours before serving.

Makes 16 to 20 servings.

Chocolate Mousse: Place 2 cups (12-ounce package) HERSHEY'S Semi-Sweet Chocolate Chips in a food processor bowl; cover and process until finely ground. Mix ⅓ cup whipping cream and 3 tablespoons granulated sugar in 1-quart saucepan. Cook over medium heat, stirring constantly, until sugar is dissolved and mixture is just boiling. With food processor running, pour hot cream through feed tube, processing 10 to 20 seconds or until chocolate is completely melted. Scrape sides of food processor bowl. Add ¼ cup coffee liqueur or strong coffee and 1 tablespoon vanilla extract through feed tube; process 10 to 20 seconds or until smooth. Pour into large bowl; cool about 10 minutes or until mixture is at room temperature. Beat 1 cup whipping cream in chilled medium bowl on high speed of mixer just until soft peaks form. Fold whipped cream into chocolate mixture. Cover; refrigerate at least 30 minutes. Makes about 3 cups.

Chocolate Frosting: Stir together 1½ cups sifted powdered sugar and ⅔ cup sifted HERSHEY'S Dutch Processed Cocoa in medium bowl. Add 1½ cups whipping cream and 1 teaspoon vanilla extract. Beat on low speed of mixer until stiff peaks form, scraping sides of bowl constantly. (Mixture will be very stiff.) By hand, stir in 3 to 4 tablespoons milk to make desired spreading consistency. Makes about 3 cups.

easy chocolate-orange cake

prep time: 45 minutes • baking time: 30 minutes

2 cups all-purpose flour	Easy Fudge-Orange
2 cups sugar	Frosting (recipe below)
½ cup HERSHEY'S Cocoa	¼ cup finely chopped
1 teaspoon baking powder	BLUE DIAMOND Almonds,
1 teaspoon baking soda	toasted
¼ teaspoon salt	½ cup HERSHEY'S Semi-Sweet
1½ cups milk	Chocolate Chips
½ cup shortening	1 teaspoon shortening
1 teaspoon vanilla extract	Whole BLUE DIAMOND
2 eggs	Almonds
1 to 2 teaspoons freshly grated orange peel	

1. Heat oven to 350°F. Grease and flour two 9x1½-inch round cake pans. Set aside. Combine flour, sugar, cocoa, baking powder, baking soda and salt in large bowl. Add milk, the ½ cup shortening and the vanilla. Beat on low speed of mixer until combined. Beat on medium speed 2 minutes, scraping sides of bowl often. Add eggs; beat 2 minutes more. Stir in orange peel. Pour into prepared pans.

2. Bake about 30 minutes or until wooden pick inserted in centers comes out clean. Cool 10 minutes; remove from pans to wire racks. Cool completely.

3. Meanwhile, prepare Easy Fudge-Orange Frosting. Spread ½ cup over top of one layer. Sprinkle the chopped almonds over frosting. Place remaining cake layer on top. Spread remaining frosting on cake top and sides.

4. Place chips and the 1 teaspoon shortening in small microwave-safe bowl. Microwave at HIGH (100%) 1 minute; stir. If necessary, microwave an additional 15 seconds at a time, stirring after each heating until chips are melted. Carefully dip whole almonds in melted chocolate; let dry. Drizzle remaining melted chocolate over cake, if desired. Garnish with chocolate-dipped almonds.

Makes 12 to 16 servings.

Easy Fudge-Orange Frosting: Combine 1⅓ cups miniature marshmallows; 3 bars (1 ounce each) HERSHEY'S Unsweetened Baking Chocolate, cut up; ⅓ cup butter and ⅓ cup water in medium saucepan. Cook and stir over low heat until smooth. Cool 5 minutes. Stir in 4 cups sifted powdered sugar and 2 teaspoons vanilla extract. Transfer to medium bowl. Let stand 30 minutes; beat with wooden spoon 2 to 3 minutes or until of spreading consistency. Stir in ½ teaspoon freshly grated orange peel. Makes 2 cups.

Easy Chocolate-Orange Cake

marble chiffon cake

A simple chocolate glaze enhances this tall, show-stopping marbled cake.

prep time: 40 minutes • baking time: 65 minutes

⅓ cup HERSHEY'S Cocoa
¼ cup water
3 tablespoons sugar
2 tablespoons cooking oil
2¼ cups sifted cake flour or 2 cups sifted all-purpose flour
1½ cups sugar
1 tablespoon baking powder
¼ teaspoon salt
½ cup cooking oil
7 egg yolks
¾ cup cold water
1 teaspoon vanilla extract
7 egg whites
½ teaspoon cream of tartar
Chocolate Glaze (recipe below)

1. Heat oven to 325°F. Combine cocoa, the ¼ cup water, the 3 tablespoons sugar and the 2 tablespoons oil in small saucepan. Stir over low heat 1 to 2 minutes or until sugar dissolves. Remove from heat; let cool.

2. Meanwhile, sift together flour, the 1½ cups sugar, the baking powder and salt. Transfer to large bowl; make a well in center. Add the ½ cup oil, egg yolks, the ¾ cup water and the vanilla. Beat on low speed of mixer until combined; beat on high speed about 5 minutes or until satin-smooth.

3. Wash and dry beaters. Beat egg whites and cream of tartar in another large bowl on medium speed of mixer until stiff peaks form (tips stand straight). Pour egg yolk mixture in a thin stream over entire surface of beaten whites; fold in lightly by hand.

4. Transfer one-third of the batter (about 3 cups) to a medium bowl. Gently fold in cocoa mixture. Spoon half of the light-colored batter into an ungreased 10-inch tube pan. Top with half of the dark batter. Repeat layers of light and dark batters. With a narrow spatula, gently swirl through batters to marble, leaving distinctive light and dark areas.

5. Bake 65 to 70 minutes or until cake springs back when touched lightly. Invert cake in pan on heat-proof funnel or bottle. Cool completely. Carefully run knife along sides of pan to loosen cake; remove from pan. Prepare Chocolate Glaze; spoon over cake, allowing it to drip down sides.

Makes 12 servings.

Chocolate Glaze: Heat ⅔ cup HERSHEY'S Semi-Sweet Chocolate Chips and 3 tablespoons butter in small saucepan over low heat just until melted, stirring occasionally. Remove from heat. Stir in 1½ cups sifted powdered sugar and enough hot water (about 3 tablespoons) to make a glaze that is smooth and of drizzling consistency. Makes about ¾ cup.

buttermilk chocolate cake

Toasted sliced almonds sprinkled over the icing make this fudgy cake company-special.

prep time: 20 minutes • baking time: 50 minutes

2 teaspoons baking soda	¾ cup dairy sour cream
1 cup buttermilk or sour milk*	2 cups all-purpose flour
¾ cup (1½ sticks) butter, softened	⅔ cup HERSHEY'S Cocoa
1⅔ cups sugar	½ teaspoon salt
2 eggs	Almond Icing (recipe below)
1 teaspoon vanilla extract	⅓ cup sliced BLUE DIAMOND
½ teaspoon almond extract	Almonds, toasted

1. Heat oven to 350°F. Grease well and lightly flour 12-cup fluted tube pan. Stir baking soda into buttermilk or sour milk in medium bowl. Set aside.

2. Beat butter, sugar, eggs, vanilla and almond extract in large bowl on medium speed of mixer until well mixed; stir in sour cream. Stir together flour, cocoa and salt. Add flour mixture and buttermilk mixture alternately to beaten mixture, beating after each addition until combined. Beat on medium speed of mixer 2 minutes. Pour into prepared pan.

3. Bake 50 to 60 minutes or until wooden pick inserted in center comes out clean. Cool 10 minutes; remove from pan to wire rack. Cool completely.

4. Prepare Almond Icing; drizzle over cake. Sprinkle with almonds.

Makes 10 to 12 servings.

Almond Icing: Combine 1 cup sifted powdered sugar, 1 tablespoon milk, ¼ teaspoon vanilla extract and several drops almond extract in small bowl. Stir in additional milk, 1 teaspoon at a time, until icing reaches drizzling consistency. Makes about ½ cup.

*To sour milk: Use 1 tablespoon white vinegar plus milk to equal 1 cup. Stir; let stand 5 minutes before using in recipe.

chocolate-almond cake roll

prep time: 40 minutes • baking time: 12 minutes • chilling time: 2 hours

⅓ cup all-purpose flour
⅓ cup HERSHEY'S Cocoa
¼ teaspoon baking soda
4 egg yolks
½ teaspoon vanilla extract
¾ cup granulated sugar, divided

4 egg whites
  Sifted powdered sugar
  Ricotta Filling
    (recipe below)
  Cocoa Icing (recipe below)
¼ cup slivered BLUE DIAMOND Almonds, toasted

1. Heat oven to 375°F. Grease and lightly flour 15½x10½x1-inch jelly-roll pan. Stir together flour, cocoa and baking soda. Set aside.

2. Beat egg yolks and vanilla in medium bowl on high speed of mixer for 5 minutes or until thick and lemon colored. Gradually add ¼ cup of the granulated sugar, beating on high speed until sugar is almost dissolved.

3. Wash and dry beaters. Beat egg whites in large bowl on medium speed of mixer until soft peaks form (tips curl). Gradually add remaining ½ cup granulated sugar, beating until stiff peaks form (tips stand straight). Fold egg yolk mixture into beaten egg whites. Sprinkle flour mixture over egg mixture; fold in gently just until combined. Spread batter evenly in prepared pan.

4. Bake 12 to 15 minutes or until cake springs back when touched lightly. Immediately loosen edges of cake from pan; turn cake out onto a towel sprinkled with powdered sugar. Roll up towel and cake, jelly-roll style, starting from one of the cake's short sides. Cool on wire rack.

5. Prepare Ricotta Filling. Unroll cake; remove towel. Spread filling on cake to within 1 inch of edges. Reroll cake.

6. Prepare Cocoa Icing; spread over cake roll. Sprinkle with almonds. Refrigerate for up to 2 hours.

Makes 10 servings.

Ricotta Filling: Combine 1 cup ricotta cheese, ¼ cup granulated sugar and ½ teaspoon vanilla extract. Whip ½ cup whipping cream until soft peaks form; fold into ricotta cheese mixture. Fold in ½ cup HERSHEY'S MINI CHIPS Semi-Sweet Chocolate. Makes about 2 cups.

Cocoa Icing: Beat together 1½ cups sifted powdered sugar, 3 tablespoons HERSHEY'S Cocoa, 3 tablespoons melted butter, 4 teaspoons light corn syrup and ½ teaspoon vanilla extract. Stir in enough milk (about 1 tablespoon) to make of spreading consistency. Makes ¾ cup.

Chocolate-Almond Cake Roll

carrot snacking cake

The last day of school calls for a backyard jubilee. Grill burgers, eat dinner on the porch and serve up squares of this coconut- and chocolate-flecked carrot cake.

prep time: 35 minutes • baking time: 35 minutes • standing time: 5 minutes

2¼ cups all-purpose flour
2 cups sugar
1 teaspoon baking powder
1 teaspoon baking soda
½ teaspoon ground nutmeg
3 cups shredded carrots
¾ cup cooking oil

4 beaten eggs
½ cup MOUNDS Sweetened
    Coconut Flakes
2 cups (11.5-ounce package)
    HERSHEY'S Milk Chocolate
    Chips, divided

1. Heat oven to 350°F. Generously grease 13x9x2-inch baking pan. Stir together flour, sugar, baking powder, baking soda and nutmeg in large bowl. Add carrots, oil and eggs. Stir until combined. Fold in coconut. Pour batter into prepared pan. Sprinkle 1 cup of the milk chocolate chips evenly over batter.

2. Bake 35 to 40 minutes or until wooden pick inserted in center comes out clean. Sprinkle remaining 1 cup chips over hot cake. Let stand for 5 minutes; spread melted chips evenly over cake. Cool completely on wire rack.

Makes 12 to 16 servings.

---

chocolate equivalents
It's always best to follow the recipe, but if you don't have the type of chocolate a recipe specifies, one of the following substitutions may work:

• ***For each ounce of semi-sweet baking chocolate:*** Substitute 1 ounce (about 2½ tablespoons) HERSHEY'S Semi-Sweet Chocolate Chips.
• ***For 6 ounces of semi-sweet chips or baking chocolate:*** Substitute 6 level tablespoons HERSHEY'S Cocoa or HERSHEY'S Dutch Processed Cocoa plus 7 tablespoons sugar plus ¼ cup shortening.
• ***For each ounce of unsweetened baking chocolate:*** Substitute 3 level tablespoons HERSHEY'S Cocoa or HERSHEY'S Dutch Processed Cocoa plus 1 tablespoon shortening or cooking oil.
• ***For 4 ounces of sweet baking chocolate:*** Substitute 3 level tablespoons HERSHEY'S Cocoa or HERSHEY'S Dutch Processed Cocoa plus 4½ tablespoons sugar plus 2 tablespoons and 2 teaspoons shortening.

---

passover almond-orange cake

prep time: 30 minutes • baking time: 45 minutes

½ cup sliced BLUE DIAMOND
  Almonds, toasted
7 eggs yolks
1¼ cups sugar, divided
1 tablespoon water
¼ teaspoon freshly grated
  orange peel
⅓ cup potato starch
⅓ cup HERSHEY'S Cocoa

¼ cup matzo cake meal
7 egg whites
¼ teaspoon salt
  Whole blanched BLUE
  DIAMOND Almonds
  (optional)
  Orange peel strips (optional)
  Cocoa-Orange Sauce
  (recipe below, optional)

1. Heat oven to 300°F. Place the ½ cup almonds in food processor bowl; cover and process just until finely ground. Set aside.

2. Beat egg yolks in large bowl on medium speed of mixer until thick and lemon colored. Gradually add 1 cup of the sugar, beating until thick. Stir in water and grated orange peel. Stir together potato starch, cocoa and cake meal; fold into egg yolk mixture. Fold in ground almonds.

3. Wash and dry beaters. Beat egg whites and salt in another large bowl on medium to high speed of mixer until soft peaks form (tips curl). Gradually add remaining ¼ cup sugar, beating until stiff peaks form (tips stand straight). Gently fold about 1 cup egg white mixture into egg yolk mixture; fold this mixture into remaining whites. Pour into ungreased 10-inch tube pan; spread evenly.

4. Bake 30 minutes. Without opening oven door, increase oven temperature to 325°F. Bake 15 minutes more or until cake springs back when touched lightly. Invert cake in pan on heat-proof funnel or bottle. Cool completely.

5. Carefully run knife along sides of pan to loosen cake; remove from pan. Garnish with whole almonds and orange peel strips, if desired. Prepare Cocoa-Orange Sauce, if desired; serve with cake.

Makes 12 to 16 servings.

Cocoa-Orange Sauce: Combine 1 cup sugar and ½ cup HERSHEY'S Cocoa in a medium saucepan. Add ⅔ cup water. Cook over medium heat, stirring constantly, until mixture comes to full boil; boil, stirring occasionally, 5 minutes. Add ¼ to ¾ teaspoon freshly grated orange peel; cook 1 minute more. Cool to room temperature. Makes about 1 cup.

ribbon of cinnamon cheesecake

At a graduation party or bridal shower, serve slices of this rich, cinnamon-laced cheesecake with coffee and iced tea.

prep time: 30 minutes • baking time: 1 hour
cooling time: 1 hour 45 minutes • chilling time: 4 hours

1¾ cups graham cracker crumbs	3 cartons (8 ounces each) dairy sour cream
⅓ cup butter, melted	3 slightly beaten eggs
2 packages (8 ounces each) cream cheese, softened	1⅔ cups (10-ounce package) HERSHEY'S Cinnamon Chips
1 cup sugar	
1 teaspoon vanilla extract	

1. Heat oven to 350°F. For crust, combine graham cracker crumbs and melted butter. Press the crumb mixture evenly onto the bottom and about 2 inches up sides of an ungreased 9-inch springform pan. Set aside.

2. For filling, beat cream cheese, sugar and vanilla in large bowl on medium speed of mixer until combined. Add sour cream; beat on low speed until combined. Add eggs; beat on low speed just until combined (do not overbeat).

3. Pour half of the filling into crust-lined pan. Sprinkle cinnamon chips over the filling in pan. Carefully pour remaining filling over cinnamon chips. Place on a shallow baking pan. Bake about 1 hour or until center is almost set.

4. Cool 15 minutes on wire rack. Using knife or narrow metal spatula, loosen cheesecake from sides of pan. Cool on wire rack 30 minutes more. Remove sides of pan; cool 1 hour more. Cover and refrigerate at least 4 hours before serving.

Makes 16 servings.

making marbleized curls

To make curls like those shown in the photo (opposite), place ½ cup HERSHEY'S Premier White Chips and ½ cup HERSHEY'S Cinnamon Chips in separate, small microwave-safe bowls. Add 1 teaspoon shortening to each bowl. Microwave at HIGH (100%) 30 seconds; stir. If necessary, microwave at HIGH an additional 15 seconds or until melted and smooth when stirred.

Alternately pour melted chips onto wax paper to create a square with a slightly marbled effect. Let stand until firm. Draw a vegetable peeler across surface to form curls. Use wooden pick to carefully lift and place curls.

Ribbon of Cinnamon Cheesecake

chocolate-mint cheesecake

A hint of mint brings springtime freshness to this cocoa-chocolate chip cheesecake. Garnish slices with fresh, whole strawberries and a sprig of fresh mint.

prep time: 15 minutes • baking time: 40 minutes
cooling time: 1 hour 45 minutes • chilling time: 4 hours

½ cup crushed chocolate wafers (about 7 cookies)	1 cup sugar
2 tablespoons butter, melted	⅓ cup HERSHEY'S Cocoa
1 cup cream-style cottage cheese	1 teaspoon vanilla extract
	¼ teaspoon mint extract
1 package (8 ounces) cream cheese, softened	2 beaten eggs
	⅓ cup HERSHEY'S MINI CHIPS Semi-Sweet Chocolate

1. Heat oven to 300°F. Combine crushed wafers and melted butter. Press the crumb mixture evenly into the bottom of an ungreased 8-inch springform pan. Set aside.

2. For filling, place cottage cheese in a food processor bowl or blender container. Cover and process or blend until smooth. Add cream cheese, sugar, cocoa, vanilla and mint extract. Cover and blend or process until combined. (Mixture will be thick; scrape sides of bowl, if necessary.) Transfer to a large bowl. Stir in eggs and small chocolate chips.

3. Pour filling into prepared pan. Place the pan on a shallow baking pan. Bake 40 to 45 minutes or until center is almost set.

4. Cool 15 minutes on wire rack. Using knife or small metal spatula, loosen cheesecake from sides of pan. Cool on wire rack 30 minutes more. Remove sides of pan; cool 1 hour more. Cover and refrigerate at least 4 hours before serving.

Makes 8 servings.

peanut butter chip cheesecake

This velvety smooth peanut butter cheesecake appeals to all ages, making it the perfect choice for graduations, weddings, birthdays, holidays—or any other time when generations gather.

prep time: 25 minutes • baking time: 40 minutes
cooling time: 1 hour 45 minutes • chilling time: 4 hours

1¼ cups vanilla wafer crumbs	3 packages (8 ounces each) cream cheese, softened
⅓ cup finely chopped BLUE DIAMOND Almonds, toasted	1 cup sugar
6 tablespoons butter, melted	2 tablespoons all-purpose flour
1⅔ cups (10-ounce package) REESE'S Peanut Butter Chips	1 teaspoon vanilla extract
	4 eggs
	¼ cup milk

1. Heat oven to 350°F. For crust, combine vanilla wafer crumbs, almonds and melted butter. Press the crumb mixture evenly onto the bottom and 1¾ inches up the sides of an ungreased 9-inch springform pan. Refrigerate while preparing filling.

2. For filling, place the peanut butter chips in heavy small saucepan; melt over low heat, stirring occasionally. Cool slightly.

3. Beat cream cheese, sugar, flour and vanilla in large bowl on medium speed of mixer until smooth. With mixer running, slowly add melted peanut butter chips, beating on low speed until combined. Add eggs. Beat on low speed just until combined. By hand, stir in milk.

4. Pour filling into crust-lined pan. Place pan on shallow baking pan. Bake 40 to 45 minutes or until center is almost set.

5. Cool 15 minutes on wire rack. Using knife or small metal spatula, loosen cheesecake from sides of pan. Cool on wire rack 30 minutes more. Remove sides of pan; cool 1 hour more. Cover and refrigerate at least 4 hours before serving.

Makes 12 servings.

cool and creamy summertime treats

Chilly and frosty desserts

are in order for the

sun-drenched days of summer.

Refresh and revive with

scoops of ice cream, velvety parfaits and

creamy pies.

Front to back: Chocolate-Chocolate Chip Ice Cream (recipe, page
Chocolate-Cherry Ice Cream (recipe, page
Chocolate-Peanut Butter Chip Ice Cream (recipe, page

chocolate-chocolate chip ice cream

For the annual block party, make this rich, double chocolate ice cream and serve it in waffle cones (photo, pages 36–37).

prep time: 20 minutes • chilling time: 2 hours
freezing time: 30 minutes • ripening time: 4 hours

2 cups sugar
⅓ cup HERSHEY'S Cocoa
4 cups light cream
6 well-beaten eggs
4 cups whipping cream

1 tablespoon vanilla extract
2 cups (11.5-ounce package) HERSHEY'S Milk Chocolate Chips

1. Combine sugar and cocoa in large saucepan. Stir in light cream. Cook over medium heat, stirring constantly, until bubbly. Remove from heat.

2. Gradually stir about half of the light cream mixture into eggs. Return all the mixture to the saucepan. Cook, stirring constantly, about 3 minutes more or until the mixture is slightly thickened and coats a metal spoon. Remove from heat; stir in whipping cream and vanilla. Cover; refrigerate at least 2 hours or up to 4 hours.

3. Pour into cylinder of 4- or 5-quart ice cream freezer. Freeze according to manufacturer's directions; immediately stir in milk chocolate chips. Ripen for 4 hours.

Makes about 3 quarts.

ripening ice cream

Homemade ice cream has a smoother texture and melts more slowly if it's ripened before serving. To ripen ice cream, remove the lid and dasher, and cover the top of the cylinder with wax paper or foil. Plug the hole in the lid with a small piece of cloth; replace the lid. Pack the outer freezer bucket with enough ice and rock salt to cover the top of the cylinder, using a ratio of 4 cups ice to 1 cup rock salt. Let stand about 4 hours before serving.

chocolate-cherry ice cream

Dust off the ice cream maker and revive the summertime tradition of making your own ice cream. Maraschino cherries and crunchy almonds dot this sure-to-please sampling (photo, pages 36–37).

prep time: 45 minutes • chilling time: 6 hours
freezing time: 40 minutes • ripening time: 4 hours

6 **egg yolks**	1 **cup chopped maraschino**
6 **cups light cream, divided**	**cherries, drained**
2 **cups sugar**	1 **cup coarsely chopped**
⅔ **cup HERSHEY'S Cocoa**	**BLUE DIAMOND**
1 **teaspoon almond extract**	**Almonds, toasted**
1 **teaspoon vanilla extract**	

1. Beat egg yolks and 2 cups of the cream in large bowl on low to medium speed of mixer until combined.

2. Stir together sugar and cocoa in large saucepan; gradually stir in egg yolk mixture. Cook over medium heat, stirring constantly, until mixture is very hot (do not boil). Remove from heat; cool to room temperature.

3. Stir remaining 4 cups cream, almond extract and vanilla into chocolate mixture, blending well. Cover; refrigerate at least 6 hours.

4. Pour into cylinder of 4- or 5-quart ice cream freezer. Freeze according to manufacturer's directions; immediately fold in cherries and almonds. Ripen for 4 hours.

Makes about 2½ quarts.

regular or dutch processed cocoa

HERSHEY'S produces two types of cocoa—regular and Dutch processed. Both are unsweetened cocoas that provide dishes with a rich flavor and color. When baking with cocoa, remember these points:
- "Dutch"cocoa has a milder, mellower flavor and a darker, richer color.
- Classic European desserts or "gourmet" recipes often use Dutch processed cocoa.
- You can use HERSHEY'S Dutch Processed Cocoa in any recipe that calls for Dutch processed cocoa or European cocoa.
- HERSHEY'S Dutch Processed Cocoa can be used in place of regular HERSHEY'S Cocoa in most cases.

toffee angel dessert

Chunks of angel cake and chocolate whipped cream layered with bits of toffee match up for a light, yet rich dessert. Keep it in mind for family reunions and potluck dinners all summer long.

prep time: 20 minutes • chilling time: 4 hours

1½ cups whipping cream
⅓ cup sugar
¼ cup HERSHEY'S Cocoa
½ teaspoon vanilla extract
8 cups cubed angel cake (1-inch cubes)
¼ cup coffee liqueur or cold coffee

1¾ cups (10-ounce package) SKOR English Toffee Bits or HEATH Almond Toffee Bits
Edible flowers (optional)

1. Chill large bowl and beaters of mixer for at least 1 hour. Combine whipping cream, sugar, cocoa and vanilla in chilled bowl. Beat on low to medium speed of mixer until soft peaks form (tips curl).

2. Arrange half of the cake cubes in bottom of 2-quart straight-sided serving bowl. Drizzle half of the liqueur or coffee over angel cake in bowl. Sprinkle with ½ cup of the toffee bits. Top with half of the whipped cream mixture. Repeat layers using remaining cake cubes, remaining liqueur or coffee, ¾ cup of the toffee bits and remaining whipped cream mixture. Sprinkle with remaining ½ cup toffee bits. Cover; refrigerate for at least 4 hours or up to 24 hours. Garnish with edible flowers, if desired.

Makes 10 to 12 servings.

chocolate flourishes

Finish your desserts with a flourish of chocolate. Melted chocolate can be drizzled into all sorts of fanciful shapes—such as stars, hearts and angels. Once the chocolate sets up, these whimsical ornaments can adorn cakes, tortes, cheesecakes and even parfaits.

To make a chocolate garnish, place melted chocolate—thinned with a little melted shortening, if needed—into a small, heavy seal-top plastic bag. Snip a small hole in one corner of the bag; pipe desired shapes onto wax paper. Let stand until set; peel from wax paper.

Toffee Angel Dessert

chocolate-peanut butter chip ice cream

Made with whipping cream and sweetened condensed milk, this ever-so-easy ice cream freezes to perfection in your freezer without the aid of an ice cream maker (photo, pages 36–37).

prep time: 15 minutes • freezing time: 8 hours

1 can (16 ounces) HERSHEY'S Chocolate Syrup

1 can (14 ounces) sweetened condensed milk (not evaporated milk)

2 to 3 bars (1 ounce each) HERSHEY'S Unsweetened Baking Chocolate, melted

4 cups whipping cream

1⅔ cups (10-ounce package) REESE'S Peanut Butter Chips

1. Stir chocolate syrup and sweetened condensed milk into melted chocolate in large bowl. Stir in whipping cream.

2. Beat on low to medium speed of mixer until soft peaks form (tips curl). Fold in peanut butter chips.

3. Spread mixture in 13x9x2-inch baking pan. Cover; freeze about 8 hours or until firm.

Makes 16 servings.

---

melting chocolate

For garnishing or baking, perfectly melted chocolate is crucial to success. Melting chocolate is easy when you follow these simple directions:

- **To melt chocolate on top of the stove,** place chocolate chips or cut-up baking chocolate in a heavy saucepan. If you plan to drizzle or spread the melted chocolate, add 1 teaspoon shortening for each ½ cup (3 ounces) chocolate. (The shortening helps the chocolate set up. Do not use butter, margarine, a spread or cooking oil.) Melt chocolate over low heat; stir often to avoid scorching.
- **To melt chocolate in a microwave oven,** place ½ cup chips or 3 bars (1 ounce each) cut-up baking chocolate in a microwave-safe small bowl or custard cup. If you plan to drizzle or spread the melted chocolate, add 1 teaspoon shortening. (The shortening helps the chocolate set up. Do not use butter, margarine, a spread or cooking oil.) Microwave, uncovered, at HIGH (100%) 1 minute, stirring once; stir. If necessary, microwave at HIGH an additional 15 seconds or until melted and smooth when stirred. Chips or bars of chocolate retain their shape until stirred.

---

banana-fudge sundae pie

Whether Dad chooses to spend Father's Day golfing, fishing or dozing in the hammock, treat him to this banana split stacked in a pie shell.

prep time: 30 minutes • cooling time: 2 hours
freezing time: 4 hours • standing time: 20 minutes

1 unbaked purchased refrigerated 9-inch piecrust (½ of a 15-ounce package)
1 cup sugar
½ cup HERSHEY'S Cocoa
Dash salt
⅔ cup (5-ounce can) evaporated milk
2 tablespoons butter
1½ teaspoons vanilla extract
2 bananas
1 quart (4 cups) vanilla and/or strawberry ice cream
¼ cup MOUNDS Sweetened Coconut Flakes
¼ cup sliced BLUE DIAMOND Almonds, toasted

1. Bake piecrust in 9-inch pie plate as directed on package. Cool completely on wire rack.

2. For sauce, stir together sugar, cocoa and salt in medium saucepan. Gradually add evaporated milk, stirring to keep mixture smooth. Add butter. Cook over medium heat, stirring constantly until mixture is thickened and reduced to 1½ cups. Remove from heat; stir in vanilla. If necessary, beat with wire whisk or rotary beater until smooth. Cool about 2 hours or until cooled completely.

3. Drizzle about half of the cooled sauce in bottom of baked piecrust. Slice bananas; arrange sliced bananas in piecrust. Scoop ice cream and arrange evenly over bananas, making sure to completely cover bananas. Drizzle with remaining sauce. Sprinkle with coconut and almonds. Freeze about 4 hours or until firm. Let stand at room temperature for 20 to 30 minutes before serving.

Makes 8 to 10 servings.

raspberry truffle cream pie

Summer entertaining is a breeze, especially when you serve this no-bake pie for dessert. It goes together quickly, plus you can make it the day before.

prep time: 15 minutes • cooling time: 30 minutes • freezing time: 8 hours

1 **6-ounce packaged crumb crust**
1 **beaten egg white**
1⅔ **cups (10-ounce package) HERSHEY'S Raspberry Chips**
⅓ **cup milk**

2 **cups miniature marshmallows or 20 large marshmallows**
3 **cups (8 ounces) frozen non-dairy whipped topping, thawed**
  Mint leaves and fresh raspberries (optional)

1. Heat oven to 375°F. Brush crumb crust with egg white. Bake for 5 minutes. Cool completely on wire rack.

2. Place raspberry chips and milk in large microwave-safe bowl. Microwave at HIGH (100%) 1 minute or until chips are melted and mixture is smooth when stirred. Add marshmallows. Microwave at HIGH 1 minute; stir. If necessary, microwave at HIGH an additional 30 seconds at a time, stirring after each heating, just until marshmallows are melted when stirred.

3. Spread ½ cup of the chip mixture over bottom of crust. Cool remaining mixture 30 minutes or until room temperature; fold in whipped topping. Spoon into crust.

4. Cover; freeze about 8 hours or until firm. Garnish with mint leaves and fresh raspberries, if desired.

Makes 8 servings.

Raspberry Truffle Cream Pie

fudgy marshmallow-nut sundaes

After the game, invite the team back to your house for sandwiches and these super-rich sundaes.

start to finish: 20 minutes

¼ cup (½ stick) butter
2 bars (1 ounce each) HERSHEY'S Unsweetened Baking Chocolate
1 cup sugar
⅓ cup HERSHEY'S Cocoa
⅔ cup (5-ounce can) evaporated milk
½ teaspoon vanilla extract
½ cup miniature marshmallows

¼ cup MOUNDS Sweetened Coconut Flakes, toasted
¼ cup sliced BLUE DIAMOND Almonds, toasted
1 quart (4 cups) vanilla ice cream
Toasted coconut and toasted sliced almonds (optional)

1. Melt butter and baking chocolate in small saucepan over low heat, stirring constantly. Stir in sugar and cocoa until nearly smooth. Stir in evaporated milk. Heat, stirring constantly, until sugar is dissolved. Stir in vanilla. Remove from heat.

2. Stir in marshmallows, the ¼ cup coconut and the ¼ cup almonds. Immediately spoon over scoops of ice cream in dessert dishes. Garnish with additional toasted coconut and almonds, if desired.

Makes 8 servings.

toasting coconut
To toast coconut, heat oven to 350°F. Spread coconut in a thin, even layer in pie plate. Bake for 5 to 10 minutes, stirring occasionally, until light golden brown; cool before using.

yummy bananas on a stick

For kids, a dash through the sprinkler is cause to celebrate. Top off their hoopla with these crispy, chocolate-coated bananas.

prep time: 25 minutes • chilling time: 1 hour

1⅔ cups (10-ounce package) REESE'S Peanut Butter Chips, divided
1 cup crisp rice cereal, coarsely crushed

⅓ cup vegetable oil
½ cup HERSHEY'S Cocoa
½ cup sifted powdered sugar
5 firm, medium-size bananas
10 wooden ice cream sticks

1. Place wax paper on cookie sheet. Set aside. Chop ⅓ cup of the peanut butter chips; combine with cereal in shallow pan or dish.

2. Stir together remaining 1⅓ cups chips and oil in medium microwave-safe bowl. Microwave at HIGH (100%) 1 minute, stirring once halfway through; stir. If necessary, microwave at HIGH an additional 15 to 30 seconds or until melted and smooth when stirred. Stir together cocoa and powdered sugar in small bowl; gradually add to melted chip mixture, stirring until smooth. Microwave at HIGH 1 minute or until very warm. Transfer cocoa mixture to a pie plate or shallow dish.

3. Peel bananas. Cut each in half crosswise. Insert wooden stick lengthwise in center of each half. Roll banana in cocoa mixture, spreading as necessary to coat banana evenly. Sprinkle cereal mixture over each banana to coat evenly. Place on prepared cookie sheet. Refrigerate about 1 hour or until firm. (For longer storage, cover and freeze for up to 1 week.)

Makes 10 servings.

Butterscotch Chip Parfaits

butterscotch chip parfaits

Layers of vanilla pudding, butterscotch chips, almonds and fruit stack up to one tantalizing dessert. For easy cleanup, layer the dessert in disposable, clear plastic cups.

prep time: 20 minutes • chilling time: 4 hours

2   packages (4-serving size each) instant vanilla pudding mix
3½ cups milk
½   cup dairy sour cream
1⅔ cups (10-ounce package) HERSHEY'S Butterscotch Chips

1   cup sliced BLUE DIAMOND Almonds, toasted
2   cups fresh blueberries, raspberries and/or other cubed fresh fruit

1. Prepare instant pudding mix according to package directions, except use only 3½ cups milk. Stir in sour cream. Pour pudding into a bowl; cover with plastic wrap. Refrigerate at least 4 hours (do not stir during chilling).

2. Stir together butterscotch chips and almonds. Alternately layer pudding, butterscotch chip-almond mixture and fruit in parfait glasses, wine glasses or dessert dishes. Serve immediately or cover and store in refrigerator for up to 1 hour.

Makes 8 servings.

chocolate-dipped berries

Bright red strawberries encased in chocolate make a delicious snack or a charming garnish. To dip strawberries in chocolate, start no more than two hours before serving. Place 2 bars (1 ounce each) HERSHEY'S Semi-Sweet Baking Chocolate, chopped, or ⅓ cup HERSHEY'S Semi-Sweet Chocolate Chips in a small saucepan; add 1½ teaspoons shortening. Melt over low heat, stirring constantly. Remove from heat.

Holding a strawberry by its green cap, dip a portion of it into the melted chocolate. Allow excess chocolate to drip off the berry; place the berry on a wax paper-lined cookie sheet. Working quickly, repeat with additional berries. Let dry. Makes about 12 berries.

Golden sunlight and falling leaves
signal a return to school and
the routines of autumn.
Fill the cookie jar with an always-ready snack
and bake a pan of bars for the weekend tailgate.

homemade cookies and bars for autumn

Fudgy Chocolate-Oatmeal Bars (recipe, page 52)

fudgy chocolate-oatmeal bars

This recipe makes a big panful, so you can cut the cooled cookie in half, wrap one portion in foil and freeze it for another time (photo, pages 50–51).

prep time: 30 minutes • baking time: 25 minutes

1 cup (2 sticks) butter, divided
2 cups packed brown sugar
2 eggs
2 teaspoons vanilla extract
2½ cups all-purpose flour
1 teaspoon baking soda
3 cups quick-cooking oats

1 can (14 ounces) sweetened condensed milk (not evaporated milk)
2 cups (12-ounce package) HERSHEY'S Semi-Sweet Chocolate Chips
1 cup sliced BLUE DIAMOND Almonds, divided
2 teaspoons vanilla extract

1. Heat oven to 350°F. Set aside 2 tablespoons of the butter. Beat the remaining butter in large bowl on medium to high speed of mixer for 30 seconds. Add brown sugar; beat until combined. Beat in eggs and 2 teaspoons vanilla. Stir together flour and baking soda in another large bowl; stir in oats. Gradually stir flour mixture into beaten mixture. Set aside.

2. Combine reserved 2 tablespoons butter, the sweetened condensed milk and chocolate chips in medium saucepan. Cook over low heat until chocolate melts, stirring occasionally. Remove from heat. Stir in ¾ cup of the almonds and 2 teaspoons vanilla.

3. Press two-thirds (about 3⅓ cups) of the oat mixture onto the bottom of an ungreased 15½x10½x1-inch jelly-roll pan. Spread chocolate mixture over the oat mixture. Using your fingers, dot remaining oat mixture over the chocolate. Sprinkle with remaining ¼ cup almonds.

4. Bake about 25 minutes or until top is lightly browned (chocolate mixture will still look moist). Cool in pan on a wire rack. Cut into 2x1-inch bars.

Makes about 75 bars.

chippy chewy bars

These crowd pleasers are perfect for autumn festivities—Halloween parties, tailgate picnics and potlucks.

prep time: 10 minutes • baking time: 20 minutes

½ cup (1 stick) butter
1½ cups graham cracker crumbs
1⅔ cups (10-ounce package) REESE'S Peanut Butter Chips, divided
1½ cups MOUNDS Sweetened Coconut Flakes

1 can (14 ounces) sweetened condensed milk (not evaporated milk)
1 cup HERSHEY'S Semi-Sweet Chocolate Chips or HERSHEY'S MINI CHIPS Semi-Sweet Chocolate*
1½ teaspoons shortening*

1. Heat oven to 350°F. Place butter in 13x9x2-inch baking pan. Heat in oven until melted; remove pan from oven. Sprinkle graham cracker crumbs evenly over butter; press down with spoon.

2. Sprinkle 1 cup of the peanut butter chips over crumbs; sprinkle coconut over chips. Layer remaining ⅔ cup peanut butter chips over coconut; press down lightly with spoon. Drizzle sweetened condensed milk evenly over top.

3. Bake about 20 minutes or until lightly browned around edges.

4. Combine chocolate chips and shortening in small microwave-safe bowl. Microwave at HIGH (100%) 1 minute; stir. If necessary, microwave at HIGH an additional 15 seconds at a time, stirring after each heating, just until chips are melted and mixture is smooth. Drizzle evenly over top of baked mixture. Cool completely. Cut into bars.

Makes about 48 bars.

*__Note:__ For a lighter drizzle, use ½ cup chocolate chips and ¾ teaspoon shortening. Microwave at HIGH 30 seconds to 1 minute or until chips are melted when stirred.

chunky macadamia bars

Semi-sweet chocolate and buttery macadamia nuts make these bars super delicious. Enjoy them by the fire after a light autumn supper of soup and bread.

prep time: 15 minutes • baking time: 22 minutes

¾ cup (1½ sticks) butter, softened
1 cup packed light brown sugar
½ cup granulated sugar
1 egg
1 teaspoon vanilla extract
2¼ cups all-purpose flour
1 teaspoon baking soda

1¾ cups (10-ounce package) HERSHEY'S MINI KISSES Semi-Sweet Baking Pieces, divided
¾ cup coarsely chopped BLUE DIAMOND Macadamia Nuts
Vanilla Glaze (recipe below)

1. Heat oven to 375°F. Beat butter, brown sugar and granulated sugar in large bowl on medium speed of mixer until fluffy. Add egg and vanilla; beat well. Add flour and baking soda; beat well. Stir in 1 cup of the baking pieces and the nuts; press into ungreased 13x9x2-inch baking pan. Sprinkle with remaining ¾ cup baking pieces.

2. Bake 22 to 25 minutes or until golden brown. Cool completely in pan on wire rack. Prepare Vanilla Glaze; drizzle over top. Allow glaze to set. Cut into bars.

Makes about 24 bars.

Vanilla Glaze: Combine 1 cup sifted powdered sugar, 1 tablespoon milk and ½ teaspoon vanilla extract in small bowl; stir until smooth. Makes ½ cup.

FIRST ENCOUNTERS

Although Christopher Columbus brought cacao beans back from his voyages, it was many years before Europeans learned the potential of the dark brown, almond-shaped beans presented to King Ferdinand and Queen Isabella. As the story goes, Columbus seized a large dugout canoe off the coast of Honduras on his fourth and final voyage to the New World. Cacao beans, the source of chocolate and cocoa powder, were among the goods on board. The Europeans were perplexed by the value the Native Americans placed on the beans. We now know that they used the beans as a form of currency.

Chunky Macadamia Bars

cherry streusel bars

Heading to a football game? Take along a pan of these luscious bars—oozing with a cherry and chocolate chip filling—to share with friends and fans.

prep time: 30 minutes • baking time: 25 minutes

1½ cups boiling water
¾ cup dried tart cherries
1½ cups quick-cooking oats
1 cup packed brown sugar
¾ cup all-purpose flour
⅓ cup HERSHEY'S Cocoa
¾ teaspoon baking powder
½ teaspoon baking soda

¾ cup (1½ sticks) butter
1 jar (12 ounces) cherry preserves
½ teaspoon freshly grated orange peel
½ cup HERSHEY'S Premier White Chips

1. Heat oven to 350°F. Pour boiling water over dried cherries in small bowl; let stand 10 minutes to soften. Drain cherries.

2. For crust, combine oats, brown sugar, flour, cocoa, baking powder and baking soda in large bowl. Using a pastry blender, cut in butter until mixture is in coarse crumbs. Set aside ¾ cup of the oat mixture. Press remaining oat mixture into bottom of an ungreased 13x9x2-inch baking pan. Bake crust for 12 minutes.

3. For filling, cut up any large pieces of fruit in cherry preserves. Stir together preserves, drained cherries and orange peel. Dollop filling onto baked crust; spread to cover evenly. Sprinkle with the ¾ cup reserved oat mixture. Bake 25 minutes. Cool completely in pan on wire rack.

4. Place white chips in a small microwave-safe bowl. Microwave at HIGH (100%) 30 seconds; stir. If necessary, microwave at HIGH an additional 20 seconds or until chips are melted and mixture is smooth when stirred. Drizzle melted chips over baked bars.

Makes 36 bars.

cheesecake dreams

In this two-for-one bar, the wonderful flavors of cheesecake and coffee blend together for a delicious evening treat.

prep time: 20 minutes • baking time: 20 minutes

1 cup all-purpose flour	1 package (8 ounces) cream cheese, softened
½ cup sugar	
½ cup HERSHEY'S Cocoa	1 can (14 ounces) sweetened condensed milk (not evaporated milk)
¼ teaspoon baking soda	
¾ cup (1½ sticks) butter	
1 tablespoon instant coffee crystals	2 eggs
	Sliced BLUE DIAMOND Almonds, toasted (optional)
1 tablespoon hot water	

1. Heat oven to 350°F. For crust, stir together flour, sugar, cocoa and baking soda in large bowl. Using a pastry blender, cut in butter until crumbly; press flour mixture into the bottom of an ungreased 13x9x2-inch baking pan. Bake 13 minutes.

2. Meanwhile, dissolve coffee crystals in hot water. Set aside. Beat cream cheese in another large bowl on medium to high speed of mixer until fluffy. Gradually beat in sweetened condensed milk. Add coffee mixture and eggs; beat until combined. Pour over the hot baked crust.

3. Bake 20 minutes. Cool completely in pan on wire rack. Refrigerate within 2 hours. Cut into bars. Garnish with sliced almonds, if desired. Cover and store leftover bars in refrigerator.

Makes 32 bars.

FEEL BETTER WITH CHOCOLATE

Have you ever sought solace in a chocolate bar? Can a bite of chocolate make your cares and worries fade away? Some scientists believe that some of the elements of chocolate enhance feelings of well-being by increasing the activity of certain parts of the brain. Whether or not this actually makes you feel better, one thing's for sure—nibbling on chocolate is one of life's greatest pleasures.

raspberry brownies

A splash of raspberry liqueur and a sprinkling of fresh raspberries elevate these humble brownies to an elegant dessert.

prep time: 20 minutes • baking time: 40 minutes

Nonstick cooking spray
1¼ cups all-purpose flour
1½ cups granulated sugar
½ cup HERSHEY'S Cocoa
⅓ cup butter, melted
⅓ cup evaporated milk or milk
2 eggs
2 tablespoons light corn syrup

1 tablespoon raspberry liqueur or orange juice
1 teaspoon vanilla extract
¾ cup fresh raspberries
Powdered sugar
Chocolate-Raspberry Glaze (recipe below)

1. Heat oven to 350°F. Coat 9x9x2-inch baking pan with nonstick cooking spray. Set pan aside. Combine the flour, sugar and cocoa in large bowl. Make a well in the center. Add the melted butter, evaporated milk or milk, eggs, corn syrup, raspberry liqueur or orange juice and vanilla. Beat with a spoon until well mixed.

2. Spread batter into prepared pan. Sprinkle raspberries over batter. Bake 40 minutes. Cool in pan. Sift powdered sugar lightly over top. Cut into bars. Prepare Chocolate-Raspberry Glaze; drizzle over bars. Let stand until glaze is set.

Makes 16 bars.

Chocolate-Raspberry Glaze: Stir together ½ cup sifted powdered sugar, 1 tablespoon HERSHEY'S Cocoa, 1 tablespoon raspberry liqueur or orange juice and ¼ teaspoon vanilla extract. If necessary, stir in several drops of water to thin mixture to glaze consistency. Makes about ¼ cup.

Raspberry Brownies

chocolate crinkles

Bursting with great chocolate flavor, these cookies are perfect for savoring with a glass of milk or nibbling with a cup of tea.

prep time: 30 minutes • chilling time: 1 hour
baking time: 8 minutes per batch

3 eggs	2 teaspoons baking powder
1½ cups granulated sugar	2½ teaspoons vanilla extract
4 bars (1 ounce each)	¼ teaspoon salt
HERSHEY'S Unsweetened	2 cups all-purpose flour
Baking Chocolate, melted	Sifted powdered sugar
½ cup cooking oil	

1. Beat eggs, granulated sugar, melted chocolate, oil, baking powder, vanilla and salt in large bowl on medium speed of mixer until combined. Beat in as much of the flour as you can with the mixer. By hand, stir in any remaining flour. Cover; refrigerate 1 to 2 hours or until dough is easy to handle.

2. Heat oven to 375°F. Shape chilled dough into 1-inch balls. Roll balls in powdered sugar to coat generously. Place balls 1 inch apart on ungreased cookie sheets.

3. Bake 8 to 10 minutes or until edges are set and tops are crackled. Cool 1 minute; remove from cookie sheets to wire racks. Cool completely. Sprinkle additional powdered sugar over cooled cookies.

Makes 4 dozen.

THE CHOCOLATE REVOLUTION

In its early days in Europe, chocolate was a food of the rich and privileged. For most people, the rich-tasting treat was an unobtainable luxury until the invention of the cocoa press. In 1828, Conrad J. Van Houten, a Dutch chocolate manufacturer, patented an inexpensive process for pressing fat from cocoa beans. The processed beans produced a drinking chocolate with a smooth consistency and pleasing flavor that could be afforded by the masses. Twenty years later, an English company developed a process for combining powdered cocoa with sugar and cocoa butter to create the first "eating chocolate." This velvety smooth concoction quickly replaced the old coarse-grained style of chocolate.

cinnamon-chip apple cookies

prep time: 15 minutes • baking time: 10 minutes per batch

¾ cup (1½ sticks) butter, softened
1 cup packed light brown sugar
1 egg
1 tablespoon apple juice or water
½ teaspoon vanilla extract
1½ cups all-purpose flour
1 teaspoon baking powder
½ teaspoon baking soda
⅛ teaspoon salt
1½ cups quick-cooking oats
1⅔ cups (10-ounce package) HERSHEY'S Cinnamon Chips
1 cup chopped, peeled apple
½ cup raisins

1. Heat oven to 350°F. Beat butter, brown sugar, egg, apple juice and vanilla in large bowl on low to medium speed of mixer until creamy. Stir together flour, baking powder, baking soda and salt. Add to butter mixture; beat until blended. By hand, stir in oats. Add cinnamon chips, apple and raisins; stir until blended. Drop by teaspoons 2 inches apart onto ungreased cookie sheets.

2. Bake about 10 minutes or until edges are lightly browned. Cool 1 minute; remove from cookie sheets to wire racks. Cool completely.

Makes about 4 dozen.

apricot-oatmeal cookies

Treat your coworkers to a plate of these oatmeal cookies updated with white chips and tangy golden apricots.

prep time: 20 minutes • baking time: 7 minutes per batch

¾ cup (1½ sticks) butter, softened
½ cup granulated sugar
½ cup packed light brown sugar
1 egg
1 cup all-purpose flour

1 teaspoon baking soda
2½ cups quick-cooking or old-fashioned oats
1⅔ cups (10-ounce package) HERSHEY'S Premier White Chips
¾ cup chopped dried apricots

1. Heat oven to 375°F. Beat butter, granulated sugar and brown sugar in large bowl on medium speed of mixer until fluffy. Add egg; beat well. Add flour and baking soda; beat on low speed until combined. By hand, stir in oats, white chips and apricots (dough will be stiff). Drop dough by teaspoons 2 inches apart onto ungreased cookie sheets.

2. Bake 7 to 9 minutes or just until lightly browned on the bottoms (do not overbake). Cool 1 minute; remove from cookie sheets to wire racks. Cool completely.

Makes 3½ to 4 dozen.

butter for baking
To assure that your baked goods have the best possible flavor and texture, we recommend you use butter. If you want to use margarine in place of butter, be sure the margarine you use is at least 80 percent vegetable oil or fat. (The nutrition label on this type of margarine will list 100 calories per tablespoon.) Any product with less than 80 percent vegetable oil or fat contains additional water and milk solids that can make your potentially tender, crisp or flaky treats turn out soggy or rock hard.

Apricot-Oatmeal Cookies

after-school oatmeal cookies

Fill the cookie jar with these homespun cookies bursting with cinnamon chips. They're great to enjoy after school or on the way to soccer practice and scout meetings.

prep time: 20 minutes • baking time: 10 minutes per batch

1 cup (2 sticks) butter, softened	1½ cups all-purpose flour
1 cup packed light brown sugar	1 teaspoon baking soda
⅓ cup granulated sugar	2½ cups quick-cooking oats
2 eggs	1⅔ cups (10-ounce package) HERSHEY'S Cinnamon Chips
1½ teaspoons vanilla extract	¾ cup raisins

1. Heat oven to 350°F. Beat butter, brown sugar and granulated sugar in large bowl on medium speed of mixer until creamy. Add eggs and vanilla; beat well. Combine flour and baking soda; add to butter mixture, beating well. Stir in oats, cinnamon chips and raisins (dough will be stiff). Drop by heaping teaspoons 2 inches apart onto ungreased cookie sheets.

2. Bake 10 to 12 minutes or until lightly browned. Cool 1 minute; remove from cookie sheets to wire racks. Cool completely.

Makes about 4 dozen.

After-School Oatmeal Bars: Spread dough into lightly greased 13x9x2-inch baking pan. Bake at 350°F for 20 to 25 minutes or until golden brown. Cool; cut into bars. Makes about 3 dozen bars.

easy no-bake cookies

Gather the kids and head to the woods to enjoy the gorgeous colors of autumn. Stash some of these chewy oatmeal cookies in a backpack for a tasty energy snack.

prep time: 20 minutes • standing time: 1 hour

⅓ cup HERSHEY'S Cocoa
¼ cup sugar
2 cups miniature marshmallows
1 cup REESE'S Peanut Butter Chips
½ cup (1 stick) butter
1¼ cups quick-cooking oats

1. Line cookie sheet with wax paper; set aside. Stir together cocoa and sugar in medium saucepan. Add marshmallows, peanut butter chips and butter. Stir over medium-low heat until mixture is smooth. Remove from heat. Quickly stir in oats.

2. Drop by heaping teaspoons onto prepared cookie sheet. (If mixture seems too soft to mound, let stand about 1 minute to thicken slightly before dropping.) Let stand at room temperature 1 to 2 hours or until firm. (Or, place in refrigerator or freezer until firm.)

Makes about 2 dozen.

CHOCOLATE CONQUERS EUROPE

Chocolate's European reign began in Spain where it won favor among the aristocracy. To ensure a supply, Spain began planting cacao trees throughout its colonies in the New World. Eventually the rest of Europe also discovered chocolate. Chocolate beverages were a favorite in the Court of France. In London, special coffee and chocolate houses were established for sipping these costly beverages. Before long, the French, English and Dutch were cultivating cacao in their Caribbean colonies—and later in Africa.

oh-so-good cookie pizza

Kids love sleepovers, not to mention Halloween parties. And these giant chocolate cookies topped with chocolate filling, peanut butter chips, toffee bits, marshmallows and almonds make great party food.

prep time: 10 minutes • baking: 12 minutes

1 roll (18 ounces) refrigerated sugar cookie dough	1⅔ cups (10-ounce package) REESE'S Peanut Butter Chips
½ cup HERSHEY'S Cocoa	1 cup SKOR English Toffee Bits, HEATH Almond Toffee Bits or HEATH Milk Chocolate Toffee Bits
2 cups (12-ounce package) HERSHEY'S Semi-Sweet Chocolate Chips	
1 can (14 ounces) sweetened condensed milk (not evaporated milk)	1 cup miniature marshmallows
2 tablespoons butter	⅓ cup sliced BLUE DIAMOND Almonds

1. For crust, heat oven to 375°F. Unwrap sugar cookie dough and place in a large microwave-safe bowl. Microwave at HIGH (100%) 20 seconds; stir. Dough should be slightly softened (but not hot). If necessary, microwave at HIGH an additional 10 seconds at a time, stirring after each heating, until just slightly softened. By hand, stir in cocoa until well mixed. (If necessary, knead in the cocoa.) Divide dough in half. Press dough into two ungreased 12-inch pizza pans. Bake 8 to 10 minutes or until center is just set.

2. Meanwhile, for filling, combine chocolate chips, sweetened condensed milk and butter in medium saucepan. Cook over low heat until chocolate and butter melt, stirring frequently. Remove from heat; spread filling evenly over crusts.

3. Sprinkle peanut butter chips, toffee bits, marshmallows and almonds evenly over filling. Bake 4 to 5 minutes or until marshmallows are just starting to brown. Cool completely in pans on wire racks. To serve, cut into wedges.

Makes 2 pizzas (20 to 24 servings).

Oh-So-Good Cookie Pizza

chocolate chip
cookies

How do you like your
chocolate chip cookies—
chewy, crispy or cakelike?
With our simple modifications to the
basic recipe, you can easily create your favorite
style of chocolate chip cookies.

cookies **3** ways

Want a chewy cookie? Use our basic recipe. For a crispy, thin cookie, try the all-butter dough. Butter melts more quickly than shortening in a hot oven, which causes the dough to spread. For a puffy, cakelike cookie, use shortening to keep the dough from flattening and sweeten it by using only brown sugar.

our best basic

½ cup shortening
½ cup (1 stick) butter
1 cup packed brown sugar
½ cup granulated sugar
½ teaspoon baking soda
¼ teaspoon salt

2 eggs
1 teaspoon vanilla extract
2½ cups all-purpose flour
2 cups (12-ounce package)
     HERSHEY'S Semi-Sweet
     Chocolate Chips

(recipe method at top right)

thin-and-crispy

- 1 cup (2 sticks) butter
- ¾ cup packed brown sugar
- ¾ cup granulated sugar
- ½ teaspoon baking soda
- ¼ teaspoon salt
- 1 egg
- 1 teaspoon vanilla extract
- 2 cups all-purpose flour
- 2 cups (12-ounce package) HERSHEY'S Semi-Sweet Chocolate Chips

For Basic or Thin Cookies: Heat oven to 375°F. Beat shortening and/or butter in large bowl on medium to high speed of mixer for 30 seconds. Add brown sugar, granulated sugar, baking soda and salt; beat until combined. Beat in eggs or egg and vanilla until combined. Beat in as much of the flour as you can with the mixer. By hand, stir in any remaining flour. Stir in chocolate chips.

Drop dough by heaping teaspoons 2 inches apart onto ungreased cookie sheets. Bake 8 to 10 minutes for Basic Cookies or 10 to 12 minutes for Thin Cookies or until edges are browned. Remove from cookie sheets to wire racks. Cool completely. Makes about 5 dozen.

soft-and-cakelike

- ½ cup shortening
- 1½ cups packed brown sugar
- 2 slightly beaten eggs
- 1 teaspoon vanilla extract
- 2½ cups all-purpose flour
- 1 teaspoon baking soda
- ½ teaspoon baking powder
- ½ teaspoon salt
- 1 container (8 ounces) dairy sour cream
- 2 cups (12-ounce package) HERSHEY'S Semi-Sweet Chocolate Chips

For Cakelike Cookies: Heat oven to 375°F. Beat shortening and brown sugar in large bowl on medium to high speed of mixer until combined. Add eggs and vanilla; beat until combined. Combine flour, baking soda, baking powder and salt. Alternately add flour mixture and sour cream to shortening mixture, beating well after each addition. By hand, stir in chocolate chips.

Drop dough by heaping teaspoons 2 inches apart onto ungreased cookie sheets. Bake 9 to 11 minutes or until edges are browned. Remove from cookie sheets to wire racks. Cool completely. Makes about 5 dozen.

holiday gifts from the hearth

Delight friends and family
with welcomed gifts of cookies,
candies and breads. Personalize the tasty
treats by encasing them in imaginative
packages and wraps.

Cookies in a Jar (recipe, page 72)

cookies in a jar

Choose a decorative 1-quart glass canister or jar to showcase this extra-special gift (photo, pages 70–71).

prep time: 10 minutes

¾ cup all-purpose flour
½ teaspoon baking powder
⅛ teaspoon baking soda
⅛ teaspoon salt
⅓ cup granulated sugar
1 cup HERSHEY'S Semi-Sweet or Milk Chocolate Chips
⅓ cup packed brown sugar

1 cup quick-cooking or old-fashioned oats
½ cup REESE'S Peanut Butter Chips, HERSHEY'S Premier White Chips or HERSHEY'S Semi-Sweet Chocolate Chips

1. Stir together flour, baking powder, baking soda and salt in a small bowl.

2. Layer the ingredients in a 1-quart glass canister or jar in the following order (from bottom to top): granulated sugar, the 1 cup chocolate chips, the brown sugar, flour mixture, oats and peanut butter or other flavored chips. Tap jar gently on the counter to settle each layer before adding the next one.

3. Cover with a tight-fitting lid; attach baking directions (see below) to jar. Store in a cool, dry place for up to 3 months.

Makes 1 gift jar.

Baking Directions: Heat oven to 375°F. Empty contents of the jar into a large bowl. Add ½ cup (1 stick) softened butter, 1 slightly beaten egg and 1 teaspoon vanilla extract. Stir until well mixed. Drop dough by heaping teaspoons 2 inches apart onto ungreased cookie sheet. Bake 8 to 10 minutes or until edges are lightly browned. Remove from cookie sheet to wire rack. Cool completely. Makes 2 dozen.

brownies in a jar

Bestow these ready-to-mix brownies on a friend who appreciates freshly baked sweets but never takes the time to mix up a batch from scratch.

prep time: 10 minutes

1½ cups sugar
⅓ cup HERSHEY'S Dutch Processed Cocoa
1 cup REESE'S Peanut Butter Chips or HERSHEY'S Premier White Chips

1 cup all-purpose flour
½ teaspoon baking powder
¼ teaspoon salt
½ cup HERSHEY'S MINI CHIPS Semi-Sweet Chocolate

1. Layer the ingredients in a 1-quart glass canister or jar in the following order (from bottom to top): sugar, cocoa, peanut butter chips, flour, baking powder, salt and small chocolate chips. Tap jar gently on the counter to settle each layer before adding the next one.

2. Cover with a tight-fitting lid; attach baking directions (see below) to jar. Store in a cool, dry place for up to 3 months.

Makes 1 gift jar.

Baking Directions: Heat oven to 350°F. Grease and flour an 8x8x2-inch baking pan. Combine ½ cup (1 stick) melted and cooled butter and 2 slightly beaten eggs in a large bowl. Gently stir in jar contents. Spread into prepared pan. Bake for 35 minutes. Cool in pan. Cut into bars. Makes 16 bars.

glorious glazed almonds

Sugar-glazed almonds make a sensational gift. Give them along with Cookies in a Jar or Brownies in a Jar. Or, if you prefer, just sprinkle them over chocolate desserts. To make glazed almonds, combine 1½ cups blanched whole BLUE DIAMOND Almonds, ½ cup sugar, 2 tablespoons butter and ½ teaspoon vanilla extract in a heavy, 10-inch skillet. Cook over medium-high heat, shaking skillet occasionally (don't stir!) until sugar begins to melt. Reduce heat to low; cook until sugar is melted and golden brown, stirring often. Remove from heat. With a well-buttered spoon, remove a few nuts at a time from the skillet and place on a well-buttered foil-lined cookie sheet. Cool completely and store in a cool, dry place for up to one month. Makes about 2 cups.

chocolate-almond biscotti

Coffee and biscotti go hand in hand, so package these twice-baked cookies in a large coffee cup or mug for a special gift.

prep time: 40 minutes • baking time: 40 minutes • cooling time: 1 hour

1½ cups sliced BLUE DIAMOND Almonds, toasted, divided	3 eggs
1 cup (2 sticks) butter, softened	1 teaspoon almond extract
2 cups sugar	3½ cups all-purpose flour
⅔ cup HERSHEY'S Cocoa	½ cup HERSHEY'S Semi-Sweet Chocolate Chips (optional)
1 teaspoon baking powder	½ cup HERSHEY'S Premier White Chips (optional)
1 teaspoon baking soda	2 teaspoons shortening, divided (optional)
½ teaspoon salt	

1. Place ¾ cup of the toasted almonds in a food processor bowl; cover and process until almonds are coarsely ground. Heat oven to 350°F. Lightly grease large cookie sheet. Set aside.

2. Beat butter in large bowl on medium to high speed of mixer 30 seconds. Add sugar, cocoa, baking powder, baking soda and salt; beat until combined. Beat in eggs and almond extract. Beat in as much of the flour as you can with the mixer. By hand, stir in remaining flour, the ground almonds and the remaining ¾ cup sliced almonds.

3. On pieces of wax paper, shape dough into two 14-inch-long rolls. Place rolls on prepared cookie sheet *at least 5 inches apart;* flatten slightly. Bake 25 to 30 minutes or until wooden pick inserted near centers comes out clean. Cool on cookie sheet for 1 hour.

4. Cut each roll diagonally into ½-inch-thick slices. Place slices, cut sides down, on ungreased cookie sheets. Bake 8 minutes. Turn slices; bake 7 to 9 minutes more or until cookies are dry and begin to crisp (do not overbake). Remove from cookie sheets to wire racks. Cool completely.

5. If desired, to make glaze or drizzle, place semi-sweet chips and white chips in separate, small microwave-safe bowls. Add 1 teaspoon of the shortening to each bowl. Microwave at HIGH (100%) 1 minute, stirring once; stir. If necessary, microwave at HIGH an additional 15 seconds or until chips are melted and mixtures are smooth when stirred. Dip biscotti into semi-sweet and/or white mixtures and/or drizzle mixtures over tops.

Makes about 4 dozen.

Chocolate-Almond Biscotti

toffee triangles

Toffee bits provide a buttery taste plus plenty of crunch to these delightful treats.

prep time: 20 minutes • baking time: 15 minutes

1 cup (2 sticks) butter, softened
1 cup packed light brown sugar
1 egg yolk
1 teaspoon vanilla extract
2 cups all-purpose flour
1¾ cups (10-ounce package) SKOR English Toffee Bits or HEATH Almond Toffee Bits, divided

1¾ cups (10-ounce package) HERSHEY'S MINI KISSES Semi-Sweet Baking Pieces or 2 cups (12-ounce package) HERSHEY'S Semi-Sweet Chocolate Chips or 2 cups (12-ounce package) HERSHEY'S MINI CHIPS Semi-Sweet Chocolate

1. Heat oven to 350°F. Beat butter in large bowl on medium speed of mixer until creamy. Beat in brown sugar, egg yolk and vanilla until well mixed.

2. Stir in flour and 1 cup of the toffee bits. Press mixture into ungreased 15½x10½x1-inch jelly-roll pan.

3. Bake 15 to 18 minutes or until light brown. Immediately sprinkle baking pieces over top. Let stand about 5 minutes or until softened; spread evenly. Sprinkle remaining toffee bits over top. Cool completely. Cut into squares, about 3 inches each; cut each square into 4 triangles.

Makes about 5 dozen.

AMERICA'S FAVORITE—MILK CHOCOLATE

Chocolate is the favorite candy of American adults. And milk chocolate is the hands-down winner in the chocolate popularity contest. When it comes to selecting a type of chocolate, 71 percent opt for a milk chocolate bar.

Milk chocolate was the brainchild of Daniel Peter, a Swiss chocolate manufacturer who thought of adding powdered milk to chocolate in 1876. This was the beginning of the velvety smooth, great-tasting chocolate we know today.

peanut butter clusters

Instill the spirit of gift giving in your children. Help them mix up these tasty snacks to present to teachers, grandparents and helpful neighbors.

prep time: 15 minutes • standing time: 30 minutes

1⅔ **cups (10-ounce package) REESE'S Peanut Butter Chips**

2 **tablespoons shortening**

1½ **cups coarsely crushed thin pretzel sticks**

1 **cup honey graham cereal**

½ **cup sliced BLUE DIAMOND Almonds**

1. Line a cookie sheet with wax paper. Set aside. Stir together peanut butter chips and shortening in medium microwave-safe bowl. Microwave at HIGH (100%) 1½ minutes, stirring once; stir. If necessary, microwave at HIGH an additional 15 seconds at a time, stirring after each heating, just until chips are melted and smooth when stirred.

2. Stir in pretzel sticks, cereal and almonds. Drop by heaping tablespoons onto prepared cookie sheet. Let stand about 30 minutes or until firm.

Makes about 15 clusters.

shortening in baking

Some of the recipes in this book specify shortening to melt with chocolate, premier white or peanut butter chips or other chocolate products. For these recipes, it's essential to use shortening to ensure a smooth, glossy texture. Do not substitute butter, margarine, a spread or cooking oil.

chocolate truffles

Delight anyone on your gift list with one of these decadent candies elegantly packaged in a tiny box. Or, if you like, use several of the options for coating these rich treats, place the truffles in small paper liners and arrange them in a decorative gift box.

prep time: 40 minutes • chilling time: 4 hours
freezing time: 45 minutes • standing time: 30 minutes

⅔ cup whipping cream
2 cups (12-ounce package) HERSHEY'S Semi-Sweet Chocolate Chips
1 to 2 tablespoons desired liqueur* or 2 teaspoons vanilla extract

Suggested coatings: toasted MOUNDS Sweetened Coconut Flakes, ground toasted BLUE DIAMOND Almonds, grated HERSHEY'S Semi-Sweet Baking Chocolate and/or HERSHEY'S Cocoa

1. Pour cream into a heavy 2-quart saucepan; bring just to boiling. Remove from heat. Add chocolate chips; whisk until melted and smooth. Stir in liqueur or vanilla. Pour into medium bowl.

2. Cover; refrigerate about 3 hours or until firm. Line a cookie sheet with wax paper. Drop chocolate mixture by heaping teaspoons onto prepared cookie sheet. Freeze about 45 minutes or until firm.

3. Place coconut, almonds, grated chocolate and cocoa in separate bowls. Roll chocolate mixture between your hands to form 1-inch balls. Roll balls in coconut, almonds, grated chocolate and/or cocoa to coat. Cover and refrigerate for at least 1 hour. Before serving, let stand 30 minutes at room temperature. Store in a tightly covered container in the refrigerator.

Makes about 30.

*Note: Almost any liqueur works deliciously in this recipe. Use crème de cacao, crème d'amande (almond), coffee liqueur, crème de cassis, Irish cream liqueur or a personal favorite liqueur.

Chocolate Truffles

double-chocolate zucchini bread

Slices of this moist, rich and chocolatey bread and a cup of cocoa make a welcome break on a busy day. Package a loaf of this bread with a container of cocoa mix and give it to the busiest person you know.

prep time: 15 minutes • baking time: 55 minutes

3 cups all-purpose flour
⅓ cup HERSHEY'S Cocoa
1 teaspoon baking soda
½ teaspoon baking powder
½ teaspoon salt
2 cups sugar
3 eggs
1 cup cooking oil
½ teaspoon almond extract

2 cups finely shredded, unpeeled zucchini
1 cup sliced BLUE DIAMOND Almonds, toasted and coarsely chopped
¾ cup HERSHEY'S Cinnamon Chips
¾ cup HERSHEY'S MINI KISSES Milk Chocolate Baking Pieces

1. Heat oven to 350°F. Grease the bottom and ½ inch up the sides of two 8x4x2-inch loaf pans. Stir together flour, cocoa, baking soda, baking powder and salt in large bowl. Set aside.

2. Combine sugar and eggs in another large bowl; beat on low to medium speed of mixer until combined. Add oil and almond extract; beat until combined. By hand, stir in zucchini. Add flour mixture; stir just until moistened. Fold in almonds, cinnamon chips and chocolate baking pieces.

3. Divide batter evenly between prepared loaf pans. Bake 55 to 60 minutes or until wooden pick inserted near centers comes out clean. Cool in pans on wire racks 10 minutes. Remove from pans. Cool completely on wire racks. Wrap tightly in foil and store overnight before slicing.

Makes 2 loaves.

cinnamon sour-cream cake

Cinnamon chips add just the right touch of spice to this tender cake.

prep time: 20 minutes • baking time: 1 hour

3 cups all-purpose flour	1¼ cups (2½ sticks) butter, softened
2 cups granulated sugar	
2 teaspoons baking powder	1⅔ cups (10-ounce package) HERSHEY'S Cinnamon Chips
½ teaspoon salt	
1 container (8 ounces) dairy sour cream	
	2 tablespoons all-purpose flour
4 eggs	
2 teaspoons vanilla extract	Powdered sugar (optional)

1. Heat oven to 350°F. Generously grease and flour 12-cup fluted tube pan. Set aside.

2. Combine the 3 cups flour, the granulated sugar, baking powder and salt in large bowl. Beat sour cream, eggs and vanilla with fork or wire whisk in medium bowl.

3. Add butter and sour cream mixture to flour mixture. Beat on low speed of mixer until well mixed; beat 2 minutes on high speed. (Batter will be thick.) Stir together cinnamon chips and the 2 tablespoons flour until chips are coated; gently stir into batter. Pour batter into prepared pan.

4. Bake 60 to 70 minutes or until browned and wooden pick inserted in thickest part comes out clean. Cool completely in pan on wire rack. Invert onto serving plate. Sprinkle with powdered sugar, if desired.

Makes 12 to 16 servings.

CHOCOLATL AND CORTEZ

Hernando Cortez, the Spanish explorer famed for conquering the Aztecs, was the first European to sample chocolate when it was served to him by the emperor, Montezuma. Montezuma drank this royal drink, called chocolatl, from golden goblets and was known to consume as many as 50 goblets a day. The Europeans found the drink bitter, but created a refreshment more to their taste by mixing it with sugar.

chocolate lover's cinnamon ring

prep time: 15 minutes • rising time: 1¾ hours • baking time: 25 minutes

2¾ to 3¼ cups all-purpose flour	½ cup HERSHEY'S MINI CHIPS Semi-Sweet Chocolate
⅓ cup HERSHEY'S Cocoa	½ cup HERSHEY'S Cinnamon Chips
1 package active dry yeast	Coffee Icing (recipe follows)
⅔ cup milk	
⅓ cup butter	
⅓ cup sugar	1 tablespoon sliced BLUE DIAMOND Almonds, toasted
¾ teaspoon salt	
2 eggs	
2 tablespoons butter, melted	

1. Combine 1¼ cups of the flour, the cocoa, and yeast in large bowl. Set aside. Heat and stir milk, the ⅓ cup butter, the sugar and salt in small saucepan until warm (120°F to 130°F) and butter begins to melt. Add to flour mixture. Add eggs; beat on low speed of mixer 30 seconds, scraping sides of bowl. Beat on high speed 3 minutes. By hand, stir in as much of the remaining flour as you can.

2. Turn out onto lightly floured surface. Knead in enough of the remaining flour to make a moderately soft dough that is smooth and elastic (3 to 5 minutes total). Shape dough into a ball. Place in a lightly greased bowl, turning once. Cover; let rise in warm place until double (1 to 1½ hours).

3. Punch down. Turn dough out onto lightly floured surface. Cover; let rest 10 minutes. Grease baking sheet. Roll dough into 20x12-inch rectangle. Brush melted butter over dough. Sprinkle chips over dough. Roll up dough, jelly-roll style, starting from one of the long sides. Pinch seam to seal. Place roll, seam side down, on prepared baking sheet. Bring ends together to form ring. Pinch ends together. Flatten slightly. Using sharp knife, make 16 cuts around edge of dough at about 1¼-inch intervals, cutting about three-fourths of way toward center of ring. Cover; let rise until nearly double (45 to 60 minutes).

4. Heat oven to 350°F. Bake 25 to 30 minutes or until bread sounds hollow when tapped. Cover with foil after 20 minutes of baking. Remove to wire rack; cool slightly. Prepare Coffee Icing; drizzle over bread. Sprinkle with almonds. Cool completely.

Makes 16 servings.

Coffee Icing: Combine 1 cup sifted powdered sugar; 1 tablespoon coffee liqueur, strong coffee or water and 2 to 3 teaspoons light cream or milk in small bowl. Add more light cream, a few drops at a time, if necessary, to make of drizzling consistency. Makes ½ cup.

Chocolate Lover's Cinnamon Ring

chocolate monkey bread

For a two-tone touch, drizzle half of the icing over the bread; then stir 1 tablespoon sifted HERSHEY'S Cocoa into the remaining icing and drizzle it over the bread.

prep time: 35 minutes • rising time: 1½ hours • baking time: 25 minutes

2⅔ to 3 cups all-purpose flour	2 eggs
⅓ cup HERSHEY'S Cocoa	⅓ cup granulated sugar
1 package active dry yeast	⅔ cup finely chopped
⅔ cup milk	BLUE DIAMOND Almonds
⅓ cup butter	¼ cup (½ stick) butter, melted
⅓ cup granulated sugar	Powdered Sugar Icing
¾ teaspoon salt	(recipe follows)

1. Stir together 1¼ cups of the flour, the cocoa and yeast in large bowl. Heat and stir milk, the ⅓ cup butter, ⅓ cup granulated sugar and salt in small saucepan until warm (120°F to 130°F) and butter begins to melt. Add to flour mixture. Add eggs; beat on low speed of mixer 30 seconds, scraping sides of bowl. Beat on high speed 3 minutes. By hand, stir in as much of the remaining flour as you can.

2. Turn out onto a lightly floured surface. Knead in enough of the remaining flour to make a moderately soft dough that is smooth and elastic (3 to 5 minutes total). Shape dough into a ball. Place in lightly greased bowl, turning once. Cover; let rise in warm place until double (1 to 1½ hours).

3. Punch dough down. Turn dough out onto a lightly floured surface. Divide dough into eight portions. Cover; let rest 10 minutes.

4. Meanwhile, grease 12-cup fluted tube pan. Combine ⅓ cup granulated sugar and almonds.

5. Divide each portion of dough into eight pieces (64 pieces total). Shape each piece into a small ball. Dip each ball into the ¼ cup melted butter; roll each ball in sugar-almond mixture. Arrange balls in prepared pan, making two layers of balls. Cover; let rise in a warm place until nearly double (30 to 40 minutes).

6. Heat oven to 375°F. Bake 25 minutes. Immediately invert pan onto a serving platter; carefully remove pan. Cool slightly. Prepare Powdered Sugar Icing; drizzle over bread. Cool completely.

Makes 16 servings.

Powdered Sugar Icing: Combine 1 cup sifted powdered sugar, 1 tablespoon milk and ¼ teaspoon vanilla extract. Stir in additional milk, 1 teaspoon at a time, until of drizzling consistency. Makes ½ cup.

peanut butter-marshmallow fudge

If you only make fudge at holiday time, this foolproof version is the one to choose. It's smooth and creamy and guaranteed to bring rave reviews.

prep time: 20 minutes • cooking time: 5 minutes • chilling time: 1 hour

1½ cups sugar	1⅔ cups (10-ounce package) REESE'S Peanut Butter Chips
⅔ cup (5-ounce can) evaporated milk	½ cup chopped BLUE DIAMOND Almonds, toasted
2 tablespoons butter	1 teaspoon vanilla extract
2 cups miniature marshmallows	

1. Line 8x8x2-inch baking pan with foil. Butter foil. Set aside.

2. Combine sugar, evaporated milk and butter in heavy medium saucepan. Cook over medium heat, stirring constantly, to a full rolling boil. Boil, stirring constantly, 5 minutes. Remove from heat; stir in marshmallows, peanut butter chips, almonds and vanilla. Stir for 1 minute or until marshmallows are melted. Pour into prepared pan. Refrigerate 1 hour or until firm. Cut into squares. Store in a tightly covered container in the refrigerator.

Makes 49 pieces.

Butterscotch-Marshmallow Fudge: Prepare fudge as above, except omit peanut butter chips; add 1⅔ cups (10-ounce package) HERSHEY'S Butterscotch Chips. Makes 49 pieces.

Chocolate-Marshmallow Fudge: Prepare fudge as above, except omit peanut butter chips; add 2 cups (12-ounce package) HERSHEY'S Semi-Sweet Chocolate Chips. Makes 49 pieces.

Milk Chocolate-Marshmallow Fudge: Prepare fudge as above, except omit peanut butter chips; add 2 cups (11.5-ounce package) HERSHEY'S Milk Chocolate Chips. Makes 49 pieces.

peanut butter chip brittle

This sweet, crispy brittle makes a delightful addition to a holiday cookie assortment.

prep time: 40 minutes • cooking time: 30 minutes

1⅔ cups (10-ounce package) REESE'S Peanut Butter Chips, divided
1½ cups (3 sticks) butter
1¾ cups sugar
3 tablespoons light corn syrup
3 tablespoons water

1. Butter 15½x10½x1-inch jelly-roll pan.* Sprinkle 1 cup of the peanut butter chips evenly onto bottom of prepared pan. Set aside.

2. Melt butter in a heavy 2-quart saucepan; stir in sugar, corn syrup and water. Bring to boiling. Cook over medium heat, stirring constantly, until mixture reaches 300°F on candy thermometer. (This should take 30 to 35 minutes. Bulb of thermometer should not rest on bottom of saucepan.)

3. Remove from heat. Immediately spread mixture into prepared pan; sprinkle with remaining ⅔ cup peanut butter chips. Cool completely. Remove from pan. Break into pieces. Store in tightly covered container in cool, dry place.

Makes about 2 pounds.

Note: For thicker brittle, use a 13x9-inch pan.

using a candy thermometer

Determining when a candy is done is one of the most important steps in making candy successfully. The most exact way to test the stage of a hot candy mixture is to use a candy thermometer. Be sure to check the accuracy of your thermometer every time you use it. To test it, place the thermometer in a saucepan of boiling water for a few minutes; then read the temperature. If the thermometer reads above or below 212°F, add or subtract the same number of degrees from the temperature specified in the recipe and cook to that temperature. For an accurate reading, be sure the candy mixture boils at a moderate, steady rate over its entire surface and that the bulb of the thermometer is covered by the bubbling mixture and does not rest on the bottom of the pan.

Peanut Butter Chip Brittle

gifts in good taste

Leave the shopping malls and crowds behind.

Instead, treat yourself to the fun of making a one-of-a-kind gift in the warmth of your own kitchen.

selecting the best food gift

Before creating the perfect gift, take a few minutes to decide what you would like to make for each person. Keep the following thoughts in mind:

- Choose gifts that can fit into your busy schedule. If the food item can be frozen or kept for weeks, all the better.
- Select food gifts that you feel comfortable preparing and assembling.
- Avoid foods that must be consumed quickly, so your friends can enjoy your gift whenever they like.
- Freshly baked goods are especially appreciated by nonbakers and by friends with tiny kitchens. The best goodies for them require no refrigeration.
- Consider your recipients when selecting food gifts. Pick foods that suit their likes and dislikes.

making a list

As you begin your holiday baking, remember to include these people on your gift list:
- Teachers and day-care providers
- Children's coaches and scout leaders
- Neighbors
- Friends
- Coworkers
- Hosts and hostesses

sweets by post

If you're sending your gift through the mail, here are some tips to ensure that your gift arrives as fresh as the day you made it:

- Prepare foods right before you're ready to mail them so they will be as fresh as possible.
- Plan to mail your package early in the week so it won't sit in a warehouse over a weekend.
- Choose foods that travel well—foods that are unbreakable and won't leak, spill or melt. Most quick breads, bars or soft, moist cookies without frostings or fillings are good choices.
- Choose a heavy carton and line it with plastic wrap or foil. Place a generous layer of filler, such as plastic bubble wrap, foam packing pieces, crumpled wax paper or paper towels on the bottom of the box.
- Pack different foods in separate, sturdy containers. Keep in mind that the contents may shift and bump into each other with handling.
- Wrap the internal packages in bubble wrap and layer with foam packing pieces. Top with a plentiful layer of packing pieces to prevent the contents from shifting during shipping.
- Consider express delivery for perishable food items. Express delivery costs more than surface shipping but significantly increases the chance of your treats arriving fresh.

beyond christmas

Although gift giving peaks during the weeks between Thanksgiving and New Year's Day, chocolate goodies make wonderful gifts throughout the year. It's easy to take an idea for a food or gift package and modify it for another holiday or occasion. Simply change the ornament, napkin or container to one suited to that particular season.

creating the perfect package

The best gifts suit the interests and passions of the recipient. With a little imagination, you can personalize a gift for each individual on your list. Such gifts are remembered long after the goodies inside disappear.

gift boxes

For inexpensive containers for cookies and candies, boxes are hard to beat. They come in all shapes and sizes and are easy to dress up with gift wraps and paint.

gift bags

Gift bags adorned with holiday and seasonal images and filled with cookies and candies make charming hostess gifts.

You can either purchase festive-looking bags or decorate your own bags. Create signature bags by using rubber stamps, embossing powders, stickers and color markers. For best results, rubber-stamp matte, white paper bags. Stamp ink does not dry well on glossy bags. If you must use glossy bags, use embossing powders or stickers.

To close the bag, first trim the top with decorative-edge scissors. Fold down the upper edge. Punch two large holes through all layers. Pull one wide or two narrow ribbons through two holes; then tie in a bow.

gift tags

Gift tags come in a variety of sizes and shapes. Look for unique tags at greeting-card shops or at party- and craft-supply stores. Or, if you like, make your own gift tags. Give last year's holiday and birthday cards a new life. Cut designs and shapes from the cards. Either cut around the design or cut a circle or a rectangle with the design centered in it. Punch a small hole in the cutout. Thread ribbon through the hole and attach it to the gift.

cookie 'n' candy-filled cones

Surprise someone special by hanging a cookie 'n' candy-filled cone on his or her door. Or, if hosting an open house, trim a tree with these filled cones. As your guests depart, present them with the sweet-filled cones to hang on their own trees.

To make two cones, start with a 12-inch square of heavy craft paper or mesh. Bring two opposite corners together to form a triangle. Cut along the folded edge to form two triangles. Roll each triangle into a cone. Glue the edges together. (Fasten the edges in place with paper clips until the glue dries.) Punch holes on either side a few inches from the top. Thread ribbon through the holes and tie to form a handle. Glue scraps of ribbon onto the cone for decoration and line with tissue paper. Fill with small cookies and candies.

themed gifts

Embellish and personalize your gifts by using fun containers and accompanying them with related items such as cocoa mixes with cookies or teas with quick breads. Pick up pretty baskets, lunch boxes, Shaker boxes, terra-cotta pots, old cups and bakeware and other unusual containers by scouting thrift shops, hobby shops, flea markets, garage sales and antique shops throughout the year.

If your recipient is a baker, nestle Cookies in a Jar or Brownies in a Jar (recipes, pages 72 and 73) in a purchased woven basket lined with a tea towel. Add a small spatula, the recipe directions and a bow and the gift is complete.

Other ideas for matching gifts to special interests include:

- *For the coffee or tea lover,* fill an oversize coffee mug or an antique tea cup with bite-size cookies. There is nothing more comforting than nibbling on a chocolate treat when sipping a warm beverage.
- *For the entertainer,* a decorative plate makes a cheerful gift. And it's even better when piled high with homemade cookies or candies. To wrap the plate, place it on a large piece of cellophane. Arrange the cookies or candies on the plate. Gather the cellophane and tie with a fabric ribbon.
- *For the cookie-holic,* satisfy his or her cravings by giving a cookie jar filled to the rim with an assortment of cookies. A clear, glass cookie jar or widemouthed canister leaves the mouthwatering cookies in plain view.
- *For the reader,* fill a pretty basket with cookies or bars, tuck in a paperback book and attach a bookmark for the gift tag.
- *For the gardener,* line small terra-cotta pots with plastic wrap and fill each with different kinds of cookies and candies. Place the pots in a twig basket and add a few seed packages, gardening gloves and a small gardening tool. Nestle the items in the basket with shredded paper. If you like, encase the basket with cellophane and tie with raffia.
- *For the baker,* bake a cake, bar cookies or a loaf of bread in a brand-new pan and deliver the gift in the pan. This makes a perfect gift for either a kitchen fledgling or a longtime baker whose baking pans have endured years of use.

index

Metric Cooking Hints

By making a few conversions, cooks in Australia, Canada, and the United Kingdom can use the recipes in this book with confidence. The charts on this page provide a guide for converting measurements from the U.S. customary system, which is used throughout this book, to the imperial and metric systems. There also is a conversion table for oven temperatures to accommodate the differences in oven calibrations.

Product Differences: Most of the ingredients called for in the recipes in this book are available in English-speaking countries. However, some are known by different names. Here are some common U.S. American ingredients and their possible counterparts:
- Sugar is granulated or castor sugar.
- Powdered sugar is icing sugar.
- All-purpose flour is plain household flour or white flour. When self-rising flour is used in place of all-purpose flour in a recipe that calls for leavening, omit the leavening agent (baking soda or baking powder) and salt.
- Light-colored corn syrup is golden syrup.
- Cornstarch is cornflour.
- Baking soda is bicarbonate of soda.
- Vanilla is vanilla essence.
- Green, red, or yellow sweet peppers are capsicums.
- Golden raisins are sultanas.

Volume and Weight: U.S. Americans traditionally use cup measures for liquid and solid ingredients. The chart, below, shows the approximate imperial and metric equivalents. If you are accustomed to weighing solid ingredients, the following approximate equivalents will help.
- 1 cup butter, castor sugar, or rice = 8 ounces = about 230 grams
- 1 cup flour = 4 ounces = about 115 grams
- 1 cup icing sugar = 5 ounces = about 140 grams

Spoon measures are used for smaller amounts of ingredients. Although the size of the tablespoon varies slightly in different countries, for practical purposes and for recipes in this book, a straight substitution is all that's necessary. Measurements made using cups or spoons always should be level unless stated otherwise.

Equivalents: U.S. = Australia/U.K.

⅛ teaspoon = 1 ml
¼ teaspoon = 1.25 ml
½ teaspoon = 2.5 ml
1 teaspoon = 5 ml
1 tablespoon = 15 ml
1 fluid ounce = 30 ml
¼ cup = 60 ml
⅓ cup = 80 ml
½ cup = 120 ml
⅔ cup = 160 ml
¾ cup = 180 ml
1 cup = 240 ml
2 cups = 475 ml
1 quart = 1 liter
½ inch = 1.25 cm
1 inch = 2.5 cm

Baking Pan Sizes

U.S.	Metric
8×1½-inch round baking pan	20×4-cm cake tin
9×1½-inch round baking pan	23×4-cm cake tin
11×7×1½-inch baking pan	28×18×4-cm baking tin
13×9×2-inch baking pan	32×23×5-cm baking tin
2-quart rectangular baking dish	28×18×4-cm baking tin
15×10×1-inch baking pan	38×25.5×2.5-cm baking tin (Swiss roll tin)
9-inch pie plate	22×4- or 23×4-cm pie plate
7- or 8-inch springform pan	18- or 20-cm springform or loose-bottom cake tin
9×5×3-inch loaf pan	23×13×8-cm or 2-pound narrow loaf tin or pâté tin
1½-quart casserole	1.5-liter casserole
2-quart casserole	2-liter casserole

Oven Temperature Equivalents

Fahrenheit Setting	Celsius Setting*	Gas Setting
300°F	150°C	Gas mark 2 (very low)
325°F	170°C	Gas mark 3 (low)
350°F	180°C	Gas mark 4 (moderate)
375°F	190°C	Gas mark 5 (moderately hot)
400°F	200°C	Gas mark 6 (hot)
425°F	220°C	Gas mark 7 (hot)
450°F	230°C	Gas mark 8 (very hot)
475°F	240°C	Gas mark 9 (very hot)
Broil		Grill

*Electric and gas ovens may be calibrated using Celsius. However, for an electric oven, increase the Celsius setting 10 to 20 degrees when cooking above 160°C. For convection or forced-air ovens (gas or electric), lower the temperature setting 10°C when cooking at all heat levels.